ALISON SCHROEDER

SOCIALLY SPEAKING

A PRAGMATIC SOCIAL SKILLS PROGRAMME
FOR PRIMARY PUPILS

Permission to photocopy

This book contains materials which may be reproduced by photocopier or other means for use by the purchaser. The permission is granted on the understanding that these copies will be used within the educational establishment of the purchaser. The book and all its contents remain copyright. Copies may be made without reference to the publisher or the licensing scheme for the making of photocopies operated by the Publishers' Licensing Agency.

The right of Alison Schroeder to be identified as the author of this work has been asserted by her in accordance with sections 77 and 78 of the Copyright, Designs and Patents Act 1988.

Socially Speaking
MT01463
ISBN-13: 978 1 85503 252 1

First published 1996
Reprinted 1997, 1998, 2000, 2001, 2002, 2003, 2004, 2005, 2006, 2007, 2008 (twice), 2010, 2011, 2012 (twice), 2013, 2014, 2015, 2016

Printed in the UK for LDA
LDA Pintail Close, Victoria Business Park, Nottingham, NG4 2SG, UK

Contents

Comments made by Teachers who are using *Socially Speaking*

I have worked alongside Alison for a year running through the *Socially Speaking* social skills pack. My group at the time consisted of children from 8 to 11 years with mild to moderate learning and physical/medical disabilities. Each child benefited from the scheme, developing eye contact, listening skills, awareness of others, social conversational techniques and appropriate models of behaviour. The above areas overlapped into cross-curricular school activities, allowing for enhanced interaction between pupils and increased active listening and understanding in lesson time. I will continue to use the ideas and worksheets from this pack in my future teaching career. It comes highly recommended.

Lou Harvey

Lou Harvey
Class teacher

I have worked alongside Alison while the social skills programme *Socially Speaking* has been developed. It has proven to be of great value to the children and staff in my class. It has brought about a general awareness of the skills children need to be taught in order to cope in social situations; skills that we often presume will naturally develop.

I have seen success in the children's interaction with each other, and their expressive language and reasoning skills have improved, as has their listening and their ability for turn-taking. All these skills can be carried over to other curricular areas. Above all it has promoted confidence in the children which I feel is central to their whole development and will benefit them in their life after school.

Socially Speaking is a programme that the children have enjoyed and the learning has been fun. I will continue to use this with the children I teach. It is a resource that is 'teacher friendly' in the way that it has been planned, organised and produced which is invaluable for class teachers in these present, pressured times.

Judy Marshall

Judy Marshall
Class teacher

Acknowledgements

I would like to thank the many people who helped contribute to this programme, in particular the staff and children at John Chilton School. A special thanks goes to Judy Marshall, Lou Harvey and Lucy Dennison. I am also extremely grateful to Kirk Bray for all his support and patience.

Introduction

The area of acquiring social skills is one that has greatly interested me in my work as a dually qualified speech language therapist and teacher. Having worked with pupils who had a wide range of abilities (mild to moderate learning disabilities, physical disability, statemented pupils and small groups in mainstream), I saw the need for a programme to teach effective social skills and how to carry these skills over to everyday life. *Socially Speaking* was developed in conjunction with parents and other professionals over the past six years in response to this need.

It is a practical programme that can be used by speech language therapists and teachers alike, in a variety of settings. It not only encourages effective social interaction but also improves self-esteem, listening skills, receptive and expressive language and problem solving.

We often think of language as simply the ability to speak. Surely if a pupil can produce the correct sounds and understand basic grammatical forms that pupil is a confident user of language? This is not always so. Using language is a complex task that involves many processes such as memory, organisation, reasoning, perception and association (to name a few). However, we can summarise by dividing language into four components:

1 Phonology (speech sounds)
2 Grammar (order of words in a sentence etc.)
3 Semantics (understanding of language, vocabulary and meaning used)
4 Pragmatics (how we use language in certain situations, e.g. turn-taking, asking questions, listening).

Some pupils may have developed good phonological and grammatical skills but lack development in one or both of the semantic and pragmatic areas. For example, look at this case history of a pupil with these difficulties.

Simon presents as a child who is very verbal and uses very clear and precise speech. However, Simon is continually interrupting and appears unaware of when it is appropriate to speak. He always answers questions but rarely gives the correct answer. He tends not to follow discussions or to look at the person talking.

Simon exhibits difficulty in both semantics and pragmatics. He is not alone. There are numerous pupils who have problems in these areas, some of whom are identified (e.g. pupils with semantic/pragmatic disorders or who have been identified on the autistic continuum), but also a large number of whom can be found in special placements, statemented or struggling to keep up in the mainstream classroom.

If pupils have difficulties in these areas, it will affect all other areas of their education and formal intervention needs to take place. These pupils will not learn the skills naturally.

Anne Locke (1985) noted that:

Language is the basic educational skill and children who have difficulty with language are liable to have difficulty with almost everything else. Whatever else they may need to learn or be taught, they will need language first.

The programme covers an academic school year, and is divided into three units:

Unit One – Let's communicate
Unit Two – Let's be friends
Unit Three – Let's practise.

It is important to follow through each term as each unit after the first builds on to the previous one. The basic skills taught in **Let's communicate** are fundamental for developing the more sophisticated skills needed in **Let's be friends** and **Let's practise**. For example, when teaching how to make friends, it is important that the pupil is able to take turns, make eye contact, place their body in the correct position, ask questions and show interest in and awareness of others. These are skills taught in the previous unit.

Cultural and social differences

The way in which we communicate can depend on a number of variables; for example, gender, social background and culture. Throughout this programme the teacher/therapist should be sensitive to these variables and adapt the programme accordingly.

Non-verbal differences often stand out the most. Examples are eye contact, intonation, personal space and directness of approach. The teacher/therapist should find out from the appropriate sources what is applicable to the pupils.

Session format

Each session has a similar format. This enables the pupils to become familiar with the programme. All sessions are best conducted in a circle that involves both adults and pupils in all activities. The size of your group ideally should be six to eight pupils. It may need to be modified, and should depend on their age, attention span, listening and turn-taking skills. The sessions in general take the following format:

1 Greetings
2 Game
3 Review/discussion/questioning
4 Role playing
5 Worksheet/activity
6 Compliments.

1 Greetings

In the circle one participant asks the person on their left how they are feeling. It is intended that the person asked will give an explanation of the way they are feeling. You will need to model this at first. For example:

Jane, how are you today?
I'm happy because I played with Chris at lunchtime.

This continues around the circle until everybody has had a turn. You may need to suggest some 'feeling' words (e.g., sad, happy, tired, excited, worried).

I am tired because I couldn't get to sleep last night.

I am excited because it's Christmas next week.

2 Game

This reinforces skills learnt in previous sessions.

3 Review/discussion/questioning

After the greetings and game have taken place, the previous session is reviewed through questioning and discussion.

Then the current session's theme is introduced (e.g., eye contact, turn-taking). The theme is discussed and role played by the teacher; then questions are asked. This encourages problem solving and identification of appropriate behaviours.

4 Role playing

Some of the pupils put into practice what has been discussed and role played by the teacher. They attempt to act out appropriate and inappropriate ways to deal with situations, while the remainder of the group identify the behaviours exhibited.

5 Worksheet/activity

This reinforces the session by adding a new dimension to the learning that has taken place. The worksheets/activities are interactive and fun for the pupils. They generalise skills learnt to other curricular areas; for example, reading, writing, speaking and listening.

6 Compliments

At the end of each session, each person must give the person on their left a compliment. The teacher prepares a number of different compliments on cards which are placed in front of the pupils. Several copies of each card will be needed. These compliments are discussed and

examples of when to use them are given. It is best to begin with a few compliments and build these up as confidence and competence are developed over time. Once this happens compliments tend to become more specific and descriptive.

It is important that a reason for the compliment is given. For example:

Sarah, I think you are friendly because you share your crisps with me.

Thank you.

A compliments chart is made for use in the session. After the pupil has given a compliment to their neighbour, the compliment card is placed next to their neighbour's name on the compliments chart.

COMPLIMENTS CHART	
Joanne	**Helpful**
Jason	**Considerate**
Miss Jones	**Good listener**

Some examples of compliments that could be used are:

> friendly, kind, considerate, thoughtful, good company, great sense of humour, funny, generous, gentle, tidy, good listener, great teacher, brave, caring.

Everybody involved with the group or class should be included on the compliments chart. If they are absent, a pupil should give them their compliment verbally when they next see them.

The teacher records all the compliments given each week in a book. This will be used for Session 13.

Using a well-structured format helps the pupils to organise themselves and understand what is expected of them. They are more likely to succeed in a situation they feel comfortable in. It is a gradual process. Do not expect the pupil to improve overnight. It takes a lot of time, a lot of positive reinforcement and a lot of practice.

All the pupils who have entered this programme have gained skills in areas they previously found difficult. For example:

> *Simon [mentioned previously], after a term and a half, is now more aware of the turn-taking process and is able to give more eye contact. He thinks of appropriate compliments and answers to greetings.*

He now needs to extend these skills into everyday situations. This will be taught in **Let's be friends** and **Let's practise**.

Assessment

Each unit has its own assessment and evaluation sheet. This identifies all skills that are taught in the unit. These sheets are designed to be discussed and evaluated with the pupil and they are written in an easy-to-understand form especially for this purpose. Before the unit is studied, ideally the pre-unit assessment column should be filled in, based on observation of the pupil in a group situation (e.g., playtimes, class discussions etc.). The pupil should be marked as:

C – Competent
H – Needs help.

After the unit has been taught, together the teacher and pupil evaluate the progress made, identifying areas of strength and areas that need improvement. The date and a stamp or sticker are put in the appropriate boxes to show the skills obtained. For example, a pupil may look at a person they are talking to in the classroom but not out of it. A sticker and date are put in the space for 'I can do this in the classroom'. If the pupil cannot do this at all, a sticker and date are put in 'I need help'.

Continual assessment should take place throughout the unit, through discussion, worksheets, video tapes and so on. A clear outline of the areas of need for each pupil should be identified so that these skills can be reinforced in the units following.

Let's communicate

Let's communicate
– introduction

This unit looks at the basic skills of communication, such as eye contact, turn-taking and sustaining conversation. These are skills which are essential if the pupils are to use language in social situations and to make friends. All of these skills are influenced by culture, gender and social background (e.g., in some cultures it is not respectful to look people in the eye), and they should therefore be considered in this context.

Skills taught in this unit are:
- >> greetings
- >> eye contact
- >> showing an interest
- >> turn-taking
- >> awareness of physical attributes

- >> listening
- >> sitting appropriately and keeping still
- >> asking/answering questions
- >> using the voice effectively
- >> compliments.

Greeting people is the first step in developing a relationship. Greetings can involve one or many of the following – verbal greeting (e.g., hello, how are you?), gesturing (e.g., waving), eye contact and facial expression (e.g., smiling).

Listening

During a conversation there is usually one person who is the listener and one person who is the speaker. It is important to be a good listener as it encourages others to talk to you and tell you things, and for any learning to take place a pupil needs the ability to listen, of course. There are many variables that constitute listening – attention, memory, comprehension, organisation and hearing are just a few.

Listening skills need to be taught in a structured and precise way. The pupils must know what is expected of them and the boundaries that they are allowed. It is essential that the skills for good listening are taught and reinforced by all concerned; it is not enough to tell the pupils to listen. The pupil who is listening well should be identified and their behaviour described by you or their peers.

The good listening skills in this unit are:
  1 Eye contact
  2 Sitting appropriately and keeping still
  3 Showing an interest
  4 Asking/answering questions (to demonstrate that the pupil is thinking about what is being said)
  5 Turn-taking.

1 Eye contact

Generally it is important to look people in the eye when talking to them, but differences in cultures must be ascertained before this is taught. Normally the speaker breaks eye contact momentarily when thinking and the listener tends to look for most of the time.

In this unit the pupils are continually encouraged to look at the speaker and at each other. Before talking the teacher should ascertain that all the children are looking and praise them for this.

2 Sitting appropriately and keeping still

It is important that pupils are aware of how close/far away they must place themselves from each other. Some may have no idea of what is a comfortable distance. They may place themselves too close or too far apart. Role play will help them find the correct distance, which is affected by cultural attitudes and personal preferences.

Generally, when talking to someone the body should be angled towards the other person. However, this does depend on the situation. In a formal situation you may sit face on and in an informal situation a person may sit at an angle towards the other person. Good posture is very important, as is sitting still. It is difficult to concentrate on more than one thing at a time, so if a pupil is fiddling it will be hard for them to concentrate on the speaker. Often they may not

be aware of this. Once again, role playing can be a useful tool in identifying this.

3 Showing an interest

This can be done in many ways, including some verbal fillers (such as 'yes', 'mm', 'aha'), smiling, facial expression and nodding. (Expressions/emotions are taught more fully in Unit Two – **Let's be friends**.)

All of the techniques mentioned indicate an interest in what the listener is saying. They suggest that you wish to know more, that you like/respect the other person, and that you wish them to know that.

4 Asking/answering questions

Asking and answering relevant questions shows that the listener is thinking about what is being said. This is a very difficult skill as it asks for relevance and the ability to know what questions/answers are appropriate for the situation. The ability to question/answer needs to be taught at a simple level and extended from there. For example, simple questions often contain question words such as 'what', 'where' and 'who'. If the pupils can ask this type of question, then questioning could be extended to questions containing words such as 'why' and 'how'.

Questions can be used to find out more information, to show interest, to make the speaker feel encouraged to continue and to show that the other person is listening.

Throughout this programme the teaching and reinforcement of questioning takes place in many role play situations.

5 Turn-taking

Normally, in conversation people take turns at speaking and listening. Often there are breakdowns in turn-taking in which people talk too much or too little. Either can create the impression that one person is not interested or unfriendly and can bring conversation to a halt.

Pupils who talk too much or too little need to be taught the rules of turn-taking. They may have difficulty in recognising the natural cues for when to talk or not talk.

Throughout the programme the pupils take turns in games, role plays, greetings and compliments. They learn to regard each other, and adults, as having equal importance in the group and find out that they should take their turn and listen to others.

There are situations when people do not take turns as often as usual – for example, when teaching, preaching, reporting news, making presentations and so on. In these situations it is important that one person takes a longer turn than the others, usually to disseminate information. The difference between these situations and normal conversation needs to be specifically taught because some pupils find it difficult to decide on the length of their turn.

Another aspect of turn-taking is joining in. The rules of joining in need to be taught and put into practice. See Session 9.

Using the voice effectively

We use our voice in different ways according to the situation. For example:

Volume:	loud – in the playground
	medium – in the classroom
	soft – talking to a close friend
Speed:	fast – excited, scared
	slow – sad, tired.

We also use different intonation patterns according to the way we are feeling. This will be discussed and taught in Unit Two – **Let's be friends**.

Often pupils do not have awareness of what voice is appropriate to a situation. Role playing will help to teach this. Continual feedback is essential to reinforce correct usage of voice.

Awareness of physical attributes

Noting and contrasting physical attributes is an essential part of becoming aware of one's own self and of others. Many pupils have poor observational skills that need to be developed in order for more complex skills to emerge; for example, recognising emotions in others and reacting in an appropriate way.

This awareness introduces the idea that we are all different and that we accept and respect people who are not the same as ourselves. This could be developed further; for example, to a consideration of race and gender.

Learning these skills is fundamental to making friends and developing positive social interactions. The study of this area will be extended in Unit Two – **Let's be friends**.

Compliments

See the Introduction, page ix.

Let's communicate assessment/evaluation

Pre-unit   Post-unit

	Skills	I need help	I can do this in the classroom	I can do this out of the classroom
	I can greet people			
	Date			
	I can give compliments to people			
	Date			
	I can look at the person who is talking			
	Date			
	I can look at the person I am talking to			
	Date			
	I can sit/stand at an appropriate distance			
	Date			
	I can sit still			
	Date			
	I show interest in what others are saying by smiling			
	Date			
	I show interest in what others are saying by nodding			
	Date			
	I show interest in what others are saying by using verbal fillers			
	Date			

Let's communicate
assessment/evaluation

Pre-unit   Post-unit

	Skills	I need help	I can do this in the classroom	I can do this out of the classroom
	I can ask simple questions			
	Date			
	I can use my voice at the appropriate volume			
	Date			
	I can use my voice at the appropriate speed			
	Date			
	I wait for my turn to talk			
	Date			
	I can join in conversations			
	Date			
	I know what I look like			
	Date			
	I can see things that are the same in myself and another			
	Date			
	I can see things that are different between myself and another			
	Date			
	I can give myself a compliment			
	Date			

Relevant information:

1 Eye contact

1 Greetings

2 Introduction

This is the point at which to introduce the circle time and to discuss the aims for the term. See Introduction, page viii.

3 Game – *Winking*

All the pupils are in the circle, except for one who goes outside. A leader is nominated and that pupil becomes the winker. When the pupil outside comes back into the group, they must stand in the middle of the circle and try to guess who the winker is. Meanwhile, the winker makes eye contact with the other pupils and winks at them. If they are winked at they must pretend to fall asleep. When the winker is discovered, they go outside and the procedure is repeated.

4 Discussion

The teacher introduces the role of being a good listener and asks what the pupils think being a good listener involves. Brainstorm ideas.

5 Role play and questions

The teacher asks a pupil to tell her/him about their family. While the pupil is talking the teacher looks away, avoiding all eye contact.

 What am I doing wrong?
How does the speaker feel?
How do I do it correctly?

6 Pupil activity

The pupils role play with a partner, asking each other, 'Who is in your family?' Both take turns at looking/not looking. In pairs, they role play one situation in front of the rest of the group. The rest of the pupils must decide whether they were good listeners or not so good and say why.

7 Worksheet – *My eye*

The pupils each write a sentence about what a good listener does with their eyes. They then look at their own eye in a mirror and colour the worksheet appropriately.

8 Compliments

My eye

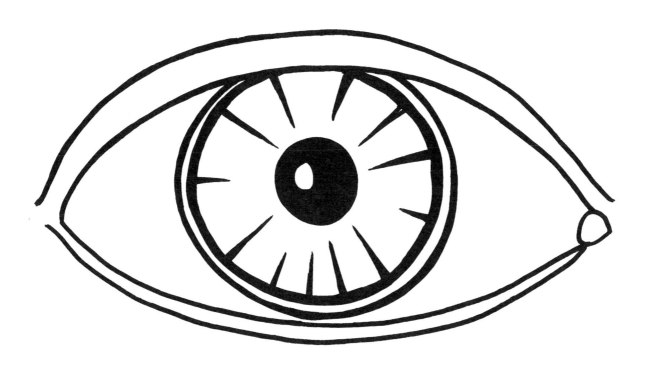

Make sure you draw your eyelashes and an eyebrow.

2 Our bodies

Materials

Plasticine, doll's house furniture.

1 Greetings

2 Question and review

 How can I tell when someone is listening to me?

The teacher checks to see who in the group is being a good listener.

 I can tell Matthew is listening to me because I can see his eyes.
Let me see if I can see anyone else's eyes.

3 Game – *The looking game*

One person starts with an action (e.g., clapping hands). The next person imitates that action and makes one of their own. This carries on around the circle. Praise the pupils who did the looking well.

4 Role play, questions and discussion

The teacher asks a pupil what they enjoy about school. This time s/he is looking at the pupil but her/his body is angled away.

 What was I doing wrong?
I was looking at the person, wasn't that enough?
How should I place my body?
Why should I sit like this?
How close to/far away from the other person should I sit?

The discussion should cover the following points: the speaker should be sitting up straight, their body turned towards the other person, and leaning slightly towards them. Vary the distance between the pupils to find the distance that feels comfortable.

5 Pupil activity

Once again, the pupils role play sitting and looking appropriately/inappropriately. They choose one situation to perform in front of the others.

6 Activity – *Plasticine people*

The pupils make plasticine people, ensuring all body parts are in place. They place the people on doll's house furniture, making sure the chairs and people are sitting in the right position and an appropriate distance apart. These could be set up as a display underneath the compliments chart.

7 Compliments

SESSION 3 Let's keep still

1 Greetings

2 Question and review

 How do you know that someone is listening to you?

Review last session's ideas – eye contact and body position.

3 Game – *Faces*

This is the same as the game in Session 2, but instead of making body movements, the pupils make facial movements.

4 Role play and questions

The teacher asks a pupil to tell her/him about what they have been doing today. This time s/he sits and looks appropriately, but fidgets continuously.

 What am I doing wrong?
I was looking at _____ and facing towards them, wasn't that enough?
What should I do with my body?
Why should I do this?

5 Pupil activity

A pupil is assigned to be fidget monitor. One pair of pupils sit in front of the class and have a conversation. The teacher whispers to each of the pair, telling one to fidget and one not to fidget. The fidget monitor must determine who is fidgeting and who is keeping still. If there is time, all the pupils have a turn at being the fidget monitor.

6 Activity – *Best listener chart*

Tell the pupils that after each circle time a best listener will be appointed. This will be the person who has remembered to be a good listener throughout the whole session.

The pupils each design a best listener chart, and then vote on which one will be used. An example is provided.

Depending on the abilities of the pupils, the best listener could be chosen either by a teacher or a different pupil each week.

7 Compliments and best listener award

EXAMPLE OF BEST LISTENER CHART
The names change each week to show
who is chosen as the best listener.

SESSION 4 Video time

Equipment
Video equipment.

1 Greetings

2 Question and review

 What does a good listener do?

Answers should include make good eye contact, have correct body position, keep still.

3 Game – *Fidget*

This is the same as the previous two sessions' games, but this time the pupils do different types of fidgeting. Pupils are often unaware that they fidget and do not realise how they do it.

4 Activity – *Video*

Each pupil has a turn at telling the person on their left what they hope to do when they grow up. This activity is videoed. Discuss beforehand the need to be a good listener.

Watch the video. Decide who was the best listener and why this was so. That person achieves the best listener award for the week.

There is no worksheet for this week as video taping may take a long while.

5 Compliments and best listener award

5 Looking interested

1 Greetings

2 Questions and review

Discuss the previous video session.

Who was the best listener?
What did they do well?

Throughout the session continually reinforce the pupils who are being good listeners.

3 Game – *Changes*

One person is chosen to be the changer. The rest of the group have to study what that person is wearing, what their hair style is and so on Then the group shut their eyes, and the person changes one aspect of themselves. The group open their eyes and try to work out what has changed.

4 Role play

The teacher introduces the role play, keeping a blank face. S/he asks a pupil a question, looks at the pupil and sits appropriately. But throughout the conversation the teacher looks blank.

What was I doing wrong?
How did it make the speaker feel?
What could the listener do that would make the speaker want to carry on talking?

Answers should include:

>> smile,
>> nod,
>> use fillers such as 'yes', 'aha', 'mm',
>> ask questions.

The teacher role plays again, this time doing all of the things above. For example:

TEACHER:	What did you do at the weekend?
PUPIL:	On Saturday I went to the pictures.
TEACHER:	Mm. [nods]

PUPIL: We went to *Pocahontas* and I enjoyed it.
TEACHER: Who did you go with?

5   Worksheet – *Listening word search*

6   Compliments and best listener award

Listening Word Search

x	s	t	i	l	l
v	h	l	o	o	k
l	i	s	t	e	n
c	n	o	d	v	j
s	m	i	l	e	k
z	x	e	y	e	s

Can you find our good listening words?

still	look	listen
nod	smile	eyes

SESSION 6 Let's practise

1 Greetings

2 Review

Discuss all aspects of being a good listener:

>> eye contact
>> body position
>> showing interest – facial
fillers
questioning
nodding.

3 Game – *Story time*

A well-known simple story is told to the pupils. This is best done by using a story that has repeating language. The story is read through. Then it is read again, but this time all of the pupils have to perform an action when a particular word is spoken. For example, when they hear the word 'baby', they cradle their arms.

The pupil who listens and acts best in this activity achieves the best listener award.

4 Pupil activity – *Interviews*

The pupils get into pairs and ask each other questions to find out the information needed to fill in the 'Here is _____' worksheet provided. While they are listening to the answers, they must use the skills of listening that they have been taught.

5 Worksheet – *Here is _____*

The pupils fill in the answers. They report back the information they have found. For example:

>> Here is Abigail.
>> In her family she has four people: her mother and father, her sister Kate and herself.
>> She enjoys gymnastics.

Then the pupils add appropriate details to the drawing in the worksheet.

6 Compliments and best listener chart

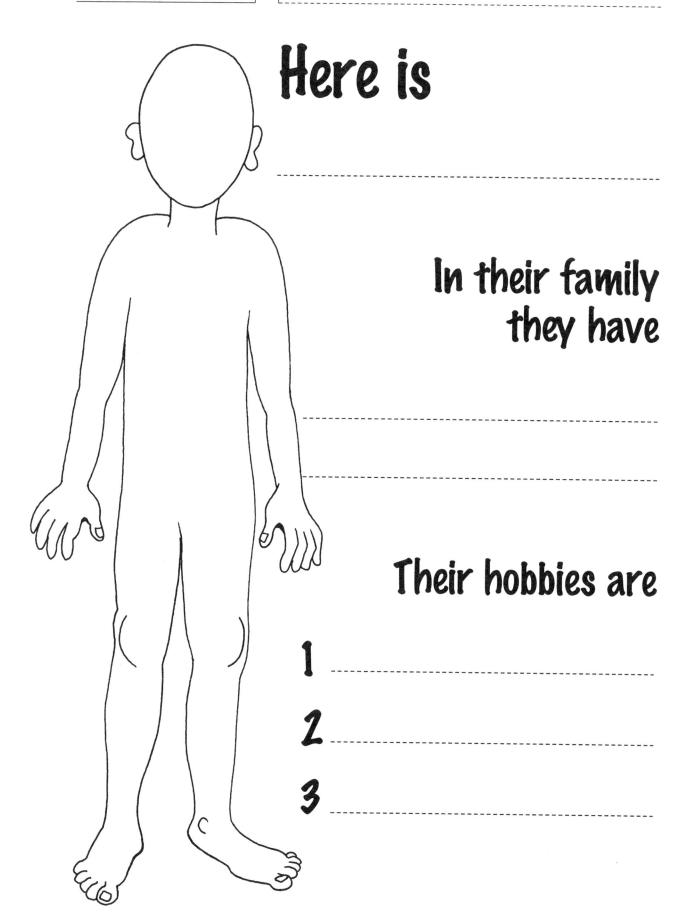

Here is

In their family they have

Their hobbies are

1
2
3

This is what they look like today.

Let's go shopping

1 Greetings

2 Review

Re-read the previous session's worksheets. The pupils have to decide who's who. Reinforce those who are showing good listening skills.

3 Game – *I went shopping*

This is similar to the looking game (see Session 2), but instead of making actions, the pupils name the items of a shopping list. For example:

>>   I went shopping and bought a banana.

>>   I went shopping and bought a banana and a tin of spaghetti.

Carry on around the circle and see if everyone can remember the items.

4 Discussion and questions

Discuss taking turns and when we take turns. Situations mentioned should include conversations, playing games, working together, sharing and so on.

Should one person talk all the time?

What will the other person think if they do this?

Do you think a conversation like this will continue for a long time? Why/Why not?

What happens if one person hardly ever takes their turn?

What does the other person have to end up doing if this happens?

Do you think a conversation like this will continue for a long time? Why/Why not?

How do you think people should take turns when they are talking to each other?

5 Role play

The group is split into three subgroups. Each subgroup has a topic that they will role play and then perform in front of the others.

Situations:

>> buying a cinema ticket

>> shopping

>> conversation

For example:

SHOPPER:	Hello.
SHOPKEEPER:	Hello, how can I help you?
SHOPPER:	I would like some orange juice, please.

6 Worksheets – *What are they saying?*

The pupils fill in the speech bubbles on the worksheets to show what they think the people are saying.

7 Compliments and best listener award

What are they saying?

What are they saying?

What are they saying?

SESSION 8 Let's be the teacher

Equipment/Materials

Audio equipment, cardboard box (if appropriate).

1 Greetings

2 Questions and review

What did we learn in the last session?

In what situations is it important to take turns?

How do you think people should take turns when they are talking to each other?

3 Game – *Mirrors*

The pupils get into pairs. One pretends they are a mirror. The other makes actions with their body and face and the 'mirror' has to copy. Then they swap places.

4 Discussion and questions

Discuss the fact that most of the time when we are talking, we take turns.

In what situations do people not take turns as often as in a conversation?

(Answers are teaching, lecturing, preaching, news reporting, presenting and so on.)

Why is this so?

5 Role play and pupil activity

The pupils are split into three subgroups, each with its own activity. The subgroups are as follows.

Teacher

Explaining how to do an activity.

Television reporter

Giving a news report. A TV set could be made from a box, the pupils placing their heads in it, or you may want to use the video.

Radio weather reporter

Giving a weather report on audio tape.

The pupils make up their own activities. They may present these on their own, or present one per subgroup.

The presentations are made to the other subgroups. There is no worksheet as this should take quite a while.

6 Compliments and best listener award

SESSION 9 Joining in conversations

1 Greetings

2 Questions and review

Review the previous sessions.

What makes a good listener?
_____ is a good listener. How can I tell that?
Let me see which pupils are being good listeners.
When do we take/not take turns?

3 Game – *Who is the leader?*

One pupil leaves the room. While they are outside, a leader is appointed. This person initiates a series of actions that the other pupils follow. The pupil outside returns and is placed in the middle of the circle. They must try to guess who the leader is. Each pupil has a turn at being outside and guessing.

4 Role play and questions

Two pupils discuss their favourite television programmes. The teacher comes up and interrupts while they are still talking. For example:

MARY   I love watching *Sonic the Hedgehog*.

TONY   So do I. Did you see it the other day when ...?

TEACHER   Have I told you about my sister? Well, she ended up in hospital when she fell off her bike.

What did I do wrong?
Why was it rude of me to butt in?
If I want to join in their conversation what should I do?

A discussion then could take place about joining in other people's conversations. Points to include are:

>> It is best to wait till there is a pause in talking. When they have paused, you could continue their line of discussion. For example: 'Oh, I saw that episode too!'

>> If you need to change the topic you could say: 'Excuse me, please.'

>> There are times when we should not listen to other people's conversations: for example, when two people are talking together in a private manner.

5 Pupil activity

Pupils make up their own role plays of the following situations:

>> Joining in a conversation about favourite pop stars.
>> Joining in with two pupils who are playing ball.
>> Asking a teacher for a spelling word when s/he is talking to the head teacher.

They should do this in both the correct and the incorrect way in front of the rest of the group. The group must decide which way was the best.

6 Worksheet – *News reporter*

Each pupil writes a news report on their worksheet, then they read it to the rest of the group as if they were a news reporter. Topics could include school events, weather reports, family happenings and so on. This is an example of a situation in which people do not take turns to talk.

7 Compliments and best listener chart

The Evening News

10 Using our voices

Equipment

Video/audio equipment.

1 Greetings

2 Questions and review

Review the previous session.

If I want to join in with others, how do I do this?
What would happen if I did not wait until it was my turn to talk?
How would you feel if others did not let you join in with them?

3 Game – *Chinese whispers*

One person is chosen to start. They whisper a sentence to the person on their left. That person whispers it to the next person to their left. The whisper is passed round the circle until it reaches the person to the immediate right of the one who started. This person says the sentence aloud and the person who started then says the first sentence aloud to see how they compare. Repeat with a different pupil as the starter.

4 Role play and questions

The teacher starts talking to the whole group in a faint whisper and carries on until the pupils notice and/or ask why. Once the pupils have indicated that her/his voice is too soft, the teacher then starts talking in a very loud voice.

What voice should I be using?
What was wrong with the soft voice/loud voice?
When would it be a good time to use the soft voice?
   (Answers should include telling someone a secret; giving someone an important message during a meeting; in church and so on.)
When is a loud voice good to use?
   (On the sports field, when acting in a play and so on.)

The pupils then pretend they are in some of those situations, and use their voices appropriately – soft, medium and loud.

The teacher then talks in an appropriately loud voice, but talks too slowly, continuing until the pupils notice what is wrong. Next the teacher talks too fast. S/he then asks similar questions to those asked before.

5 Pupil activity

In pairs, the pupils practise asking and telling each other what they will do at the weekend. They practise two versions; one is to be either too fast/slow/loud or soft, and the other is to be at the right speed and volume.

This will be video or audio taped, and watched or listened to by all at the end of the session. A discussion could take place about how well people were using their voices to convey a message.

6 Compliments and best listener chart

SESSION 11 Myself

1 Greetings

2 Questions and review

Review the previous session.

When do we take/not take turns?
How do I know that someone is listening to me?
When and how is it appropriate to join in with others?

3 Game – *Guess who?*

Each pupil has to describe another pupil in the group by using two descriptive elements. For example: 'They have brown hair and are wearing a blue top.' The pupil who is being described puts their hand up. If they are correct, they then describe another pupil and the game continues.

4 Discussion

There is a short discussion about what each pupil looks like. Each describes what they look like to the rest of the group. The description should include:

>> height (tall, short etc.)
>> hair (colour, length, style)
>> eye colour
>> skin colour.

5 Worksheet – *Guess who?*

Each pupil fills in the worksheet, describing themselves without any help from others with what they actually look like. Then the worksheets are read out to the group, and the pupils have to guess whom each one describes.

6 Compliments and best listener award

Guess who?

Hair

Colour _____

Length _____

Style _____

Eye colour

_____

Skin colour

_____

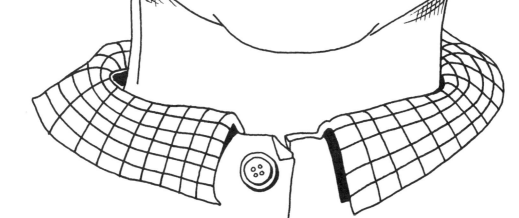

12 I am unique

Materials

Objects for the game.

---

1 Greetings

2 Review

Either the pupils or the teacher read out the worksheets from the previous session. The pupils must work out whom each one describes.

3 Game – *Same/different*

A bag is full of similar objects, for example:

>> a big blue plate
>> a small blue plate
>> a blunt blue pencil
>> a short blue pencil
>> a long blue pencil.

The pupils each take two objects out of the bag. They have to state in turn one thing that is the same about them and one thing that is different. For example, a pupil picks out a big blue plate and a long blue pencil. They could say, 'The thing that is the same is that they are both blue, and the thing that is different is you eat off one and you draw with the other.'

4 Questions and discussion

What is something that is different about you and another pupil/adult?
What is something that is the same?

You may need to model this for the pupils as some may find it extremely difficult.

Go round the group and see if each pupil can find one thing similar and one thing different about themselves and the person next to them; for example: 'We both have blue eyes, but I have blonde hair and she has brown.'

The discussion should cover the fact that we are all different and unique and that makes us special. Not only do we all look different but we are all different inside – that is what makes us, us.

You can bring up issues such as different backgrounds, cultures, disabilities, religions, gender and so on. That will depend on your group and how comfortable you feel about doing this.

5 Worksheet – *I am unique*

In pairs, the pupils fill in the worksheet. These are then read to the rest of the group.

6 Compliments and best listener award

I am unique!

We are _____

and _____

Here are two things
that are different about us.

_____

_____

Here are two things
that are the same about us.

_____

_____

There is no one
the same as me!

39

13 Here I am

Equipment/Materials

Projector, coloured cartridge paper (including black).

1 Greetings

2 Review

Read out the worksheets from the previous session in pairs. The pupils have to guess which worksheet belongs to whom.

3 Game – *Simon says*

The pupils stand in a circle. One is chosen as leader, and stands in the middle. The rest follow all instructions given by the leader that begin with the words 'Simon says', ignoring any others. Anyone who does not respond correctly is out and sits down.

4 Discussion

Each person is told two compliments that were paid to them in previous sessions. The rest of the group gives the person three more compliments. They are all put on the board. This is to include everyone, adults and pupils.

Using an overhead projector, a silhouette is made of each person's head with black cartridge paper. Each person writes their compliment on different coloured paper and sticks it on the silhouette head below the title 'What others think of me'. An example is provided. These are then displayed on the wall. Try to provide a brightly coloured background.

5 Compliments and best listener award

Instead of giving each other a compliment, today the pupils think of one compliment they would give themselves. For example: 'I am friendly.'

What others think of me

Thoughtful

Good listener

Friendly

Considerate

Kind

UNIT TWO

Let's
be friends

Let's be friends – introduction

The ability to communicate effectively with others is essential in all sectors of life, especially in developing relationships and friendships. In Unit One we looked at the basic skills of communication, such as eye contact, turn-taking, active listening and sustaining a conversation. These skills are needed before any relationship can be truly developed, and it is essential that Unit One is taught first.

Constant review of those communication skills is required. To aid this each pupil is assigned their own specific skill to develop. This is discussed and the pupil and teacher together decide on the area that is to be developed. This is written on an individual chart and placed on the wall together with a statement of the reward for reaching the agreed target. At the beginning of each session the aims should be discussed and at the end they should be evaluated. If the pupil has achieved their task, then they receive a sticker for their chart. The sticker could resemble their aim. For example:

>> 'to look at people when talking' – a picture of an eye
>> 'to ask more questions' – a picture of a question mark
>> 'to sit still' – a person sitting in a chair.

The pictures could be drawn by the teacher on coloured sticky paper and then stuck on the chart, or you may want to purchase ready-made stickers from suppliers. Once the pupil has reached the target (e.g., five stickers), then they immediately receive a reward. This reward should be decided upon in Session 1. The chart will replace the best listener award of the previous unit. Once the pupils have achieved their target and gained their reward, a new target and reward should be decided on.

This is one of many types of reinforcement charts, certificates, vouchers and so on used in this unit. All aid positive social interactions and enhance self-esteem.

Now that the pupils are aware of the basic skills and hopefully will use these, they are ready to learn how to develop friendships and relationships. To be able to do this the pupils need to look at things from another perspective, as Curry and Bromfield (1994) noted:

> Children need to understand how friendships are developed and maintained and in order for this to happen they must also acquire the ability to look at things from another's point of view.

Often pupils with learning disabilities find it difficult to come to terms with their own emotions and thoughts, let alone another's. It is essential that they learn to identify their own feelings, so they can then develop the ability to understand how others feel and the effect their behaviour has on others.

Emotions

The unit begins by looking at emotions. Happiness, sadness, anger and excitement are looked at in depth and other emotions (such as worry, surprise, joy etc.) are discussed and role played.

The pupils learn to identify situations and people that evoke certain emotions. Not only do they identify these in themselves, but also in others. These issues are raised through discussion, questioning, interviewing, games, role playing, art activities and identification of emotions through body language, music and intonation. Pupils learn that emotions are not only expressed through words, but also through other means. For example:

>> happy – smiling
  laughing
  eyes wide open and shining
  body upright
  increased expression in voice.

They also associate these with picture symbols (provided in Session 2), noting specific features that help them determine the emotion.

Often pupils with learning difficulties find it difficult to see the world through other people's eyes and to understand that people think differently from themselves. All these activities aim to teach these pupils to learn how others think.

Sessions 2 to 6 emphasise the need to express/articulate one's feelings and to be aware of the feelings of others. The pupils learn that they are not alone and that others experience similar emotions to theirs.

Activities reinforce the identification of emotions and the effects these emotions have on ourselves and others. Discussion and problem solving activities try to elicit appropriate outcomes and ways to deal with situations that present themselves. Learning to respond to others appropriately, making relevant comments and questions, is highlighted.

Making friends

Hopefully the pupils are now able to understand a little about themselves and the way they interact with others. They should be aware of the needs of others in order to be able to build up positive relationships. Interactions throughout this programme give the pupils models for positive behaviour. Success in this will raise their self-esteem. If a pupil has a high level of self-esteem, then this should make them more confident in social situations. They will like themselves and realise that others will like them too.

Some pupils, however, need to be taught not just what friendship entails but ways to make and keep friends. It doesn't always come naturally! Sessions 7 to 12 look at what a friend is; how to meet, make and keep friends (including how to make and maintain conversational topics); how to greet friends; and identification of things friends should and should not do. The greetings section is expanded so that the pupils learn to make relevant comments and to ask a range of questions.

Each pupil will complete their own friendship

book over the duration of these sessions. This book will include worksheets, vouchers, games and a friendship certificate. It would be a good idea to issue each pupil with a folder to keep the components in. At the end of the unit the pupils should staple these together to make the book. Activities involve developing interactive skills in the classroom and playground and at home. Session 12 includes an award-giving ceremony. It is hoped that parents, head teachers and significant others can be invited so this can be made into a very important occasion.

It is emphasised, as in the previous unit, that we are not all the same. The pupils learn to recognise and build on the similarities they have and to respect the differences between them.

This unit further develops the social skills of the pupils you work with. These skills enable them to be more effective in developing relationships with their peers, parents, others in school and people in the wider community. Not only does this develop relationships but it enhances self-esteem, so that the pupils learn to live and work positively with others.

This unit varies from Unit One in that there is more variety of activities and not so many role plays.

Let's be friends
assessment/evaluation

Pre-unit   Post-unit

	Skills	I need help	I can do this in the classroom	I can do this out of the classroom
	I know what makes me happy			
	Date			
	I know what makes others happy			
	Date			
	I can show I'm happy by using my voice			
	Date			
	I can show I'm happy by using my face			
	Date			
	I can show I'm happy by using my body			
	Date			
	I know what makes me sad			
	Date			
	I know what makes others sad			
	Date			
	I can show I'm sad by using my voice			
	Date			
	I can show I'm sad by using my face			
	Date			
	I can show I'm sad by using my body			
	Date			

Let's be friends
assessment/evaluation

Pre-unit   Post-unit

	Skills	I need help	I can do this in the classroom	I can do this out of the classroom
	I know what makes me excited			
	Date			
	I know what makes others excited			
	Date			
	I can show I'm excited by using my voice			
	Date			
	I can show I'm excited by using my face			
	Date			
	I can show I'm excited by using my body			
	Date			
	I know what makes me angry			
	Date			
	I know what makes others angry			
	Date			
	I can show I'm angry by using my voice			
	Date			
	I can show I'm angry by using my face			
	Date			
	I can show I'm angry by using my body			
	Date			

Let's be friends
assessment/evaluation

Pre-unit   **Post-unit**

	Skills	I need help	I can do this in the classroom	I can do this out of the classroom
	I can respond appropriately to how another is feeling			
	Date			
	I can keep a conversation going by making relevant comments			
	Date			
	I can keep a conversation going by asking relevant questions			
	Date			
	I can introduce a topic appropriate to the situation			
	Date			
	I know what a friend is			
	Date			
	I know what friends should not do			
	Date			
	I am a good friend			
	Date			

Let's be friends
assessment/evaluation

Pre-unit   **Post-unit**

	Skills	I need help	I can do this in the classroom	I can do this out of the classroom
	I know how to make a new friend by introducing myself			
	Date			
	I know how to make a new friend by inviting them to play			
	Date			
	I know how to make a new friend by asking them questions			
	Date			
	I know how to greet friends after a short time			
	Date			
	I know how to greet friends after a long time			
	Date			

Relevant information:

Materials

Stickers for game.

---

1 Greetings

2 Review

Review all aspects of being a good communicator:

>> eye contact
>> body position
>> showing interest – face
>> >> fillers
>> >> questioning
>> >> nodding
>> taking turns
>> joining in with others
>> using an appropriate voice.

Reinforcement chart

Discussion takes place to decide on the skills each pupil needs to develop (see introductory notes to this unit, page 45). The pupils should decide on their rewards at this time. Examples of rewards could be:

>> helping the secretary
>> playing on the computer
>> going for a walk around the school with another pupil.

3 Game – *Stickers*

A sticker showing an object is placed in the middle of every person's forehead, just above the eyes. You can use plain white stickers to draw pictures of objects on; for example, cat, ball and house. Each person assumes the name of their object and must say 'hello' to the person next door. For example:

BALL: Hello, car.
CAR: Hello, ball.

The first person then asks the other to say 'hello' to the next member of the circle. For example:

BALL:	Say 'hello' to dog.
CAR:	Hello, dog.
DOG:	Hello, car.
CAR:	Say 'hello' to ring. [and so on]

This continues until everyone has said 'hello'. It is hoped that the pupils will maintain eye contact throughout the greeting. You can make this harder by choosing anybody to say 'hello' to rather than going round the circle.

4 Discussion

Discuss the idea that we are all unique – no one is the same as anyone else. Can the pupils think of a compliment to give themselves?

Discuss the fact that we are all special and unique. This should cover the following points. We all have different like/dislikes, hobbies and emotions. This term we are going to find out about all of these, not just about our own but also about those of our friends, teachers, family and so on. All of this helps us to learn how friendships are developed and maintained.

5 Worksheet – *All about me*

The pupils fill in the worksheet on their own. When completed, these are read out one at a time to the rest of the group. Each time a point is made, the teacher asks the other pupils if they have similar likes, emotions and so on.

For example, one pupil says, 'I'm good at writing.'

The teacher asks, 'Who else thinks they are good at writing?' This introduces the idea that people are all unique but they do have thing in common.

6 Compliments and reinforcement chart

This is me

My name is

One thing I am good at is

I like eating

I like playing

One thing that makes me happy is

One thing that makes me sad is

2 Happiness

Materials

Cards and containers for
activity.

1 Greetings

2 Questions and discussion

Review the aims set in the previous session.

Are we all the same?
What makes each of us happy?

Each person gives an example of one thing that makes them happy.

Does the same thing make everybody happy?
How do we show others that we are happy?

Answers might include:

>> smiling
laughing
>> eyes wide open and shining
>> body upright
>> raised expression in voice.

The sheet of picture symbols provided should be presented. This will be used later, on the
emotion display board that will be started in Session 4.

Can the pupils think of other words that they could use instead
of 'happy'?

Answers might include:

>> pleased
>> glad
>> contented.

3   Game and discussion – *Rice pudding*

All the pupils, in a circle, ask a nominated pupil questions. The pupil who is questioned must answer 'rice pudding' only; if they smile or laugh they must give up their turn.

Make sure that the pupils understand that when people laugh or smile it can be contagious, just as in the game of 'Rice pudding'. It is difficult not to laugh or smile if others around you are doing it.

What makes others happy?

The pupils get into pairs and discuss what makes their parents, teachers and classmates happy. Once discussed, these ideas are reported back to the group and then recorded on the board.

4   Activity

Each pupil writes their name on a card. On two other cards they write two things they can do that make others happy. The cards are put into two separate containers – one marked 'NAMES' and the other marked 'HAPPINESS'. Everyone involved in the circle should have their name in the name container. Each person then takes out a name and a happiness card. They will have to make the named person happy by doing what it says on the card every day at school.

These should then be recorded on a chart so that everybody can see them. For example:

> JOHN: I will make Carl happy by playing with him at lunchtime.
>
> MRS SMITH: I will make Simon happy by paying him compliments.
>
> JANE: I will make Louise happy by smiling at her.

A happiness chart with everybody's name on it is then shown to the group (an example is provided). If the person carries out their happiness task every day they will get a star on the chart at the beginning of each session. This must be done honestly with both the adult and the pupils involved telling the truth about whether or not they have carried out the task correctly. If the person is honest and says they have not carried out their task correctly, they get a star to wear for being honest. The pupils should be made to realise that it is better to be honest than not, and they should feel safe enough to tell the truth.

This will be continued every week for the next five weeks. If any of the pupils has four stars on their chart at the end of this time they will immediately receive a happiness certificate. A certificate is provided.

5   Compliments and reinforcement chart

Picture symbols

Happy

Sad

Excited

Angry

Surprised

Scared

Worried

Hurt

Happiness Chart

LEROY	I will talk to Sulinder every day.	
MARIA	I will say 'Good morning' to Mrs Graham.	
MRS GRAHAM	I will give Jack plenty of compliments.	
STEVEN	I will play tennis with Maria.	
JACK	I will help Leroy in maths.	
SULINDER	I will read a book with Steven.	

Unit Two, Session 2

Happiness Certificate

This is awarded to

SESSION 3 Sadness

> **Materials**
>
> Cards for game, picture symbols (Session 2), happiness chart (Session 2).

1 Greetings

2 Review

Review aims.

The happiness chart is displayed. Each pupil's task is discussed in turn and a star is given if the pupil has been honest and/or made the other person named happy.

3 Game – *Happy animals*

Each child chooses an animal that they consider to be happy. Their choice is recorded on a card with a reason why the animal is happy. For example:

> Cat – I would be happy if I could lie and stretch in the sun all day.

The cards are collected and read out by the teacher. The pupils have to guess who chose each particular animal.

4 Discussion

Everyone should name one thing that makes them sad.

 How do you show that you are sad?

Answers might include:

- >> crying
- >> frowning
- >> sulking
- >> eyes are small and turned down
- >> body is lowered/head is down
- >> voice is quiet and slow.

The picture symbol for 'sad' is shown. Can the pupils think of other words for 'sad'? For example: down, unhappy, gloomy.

What makes other sad?
What may we do that makes others sad?
How can we change this?
How do we make things better?

Answers might include:

>> say 'sorry'
>> write a letter
>> give a present (e.g., flowers)
>> give a hug and smile
>> do something special (e.g., make a cup of tea, clean your bedroom).

5 Worksheet – *How do you feel?*

The pupils fill in the first part of the worksheet by putting ticks in the appropriate column. For the second part, they should write down one thing that makes themselves, their parents and their teacher happy or sad.

6 Activity

This is a continuation of the activity in Session 2. Each person takes a new name and happiness card for the following session. These are recorded and displayed so everyone can see them.

7 Compliments and reinforcement chart

How do you feel?

<····· happy or sad ·····>

		😊	😢
1	Someone called me names.		
2	My cat died.		
3	It is my birthday tomorrow.		
4	Grandma is visiting today.		
5	We are going on holiday.		
6	I have cut my foot.		
7	I am not allowed to go to the cinema.		
8	My mum just gave me a hug.		
9	My teacher gave me a star.		

How do you make others happy/sad?

	😊	😢
Parents		
Teacher		
Classmates		

SESSION **4 Excitement**

Materials

Happiness chart (Session 2),
cards for discussion and for
first activity, picture symbols
(Session 2).

---

1 Greetings

2 Review

Review aims.

Next, the happiness chart is displayed. Each pupil is given a star if they have been honest and/or have made another happy.

3 Game – *That's good news*

The pupils are each given a card that has a happy or sad situation written on it. Ten of these are provided.

Each pupil reads their card to whoever is sitting next to them, using the first person, with the appropriate expression and body language. The other pupil must respond in an appropriate way using the correct expression and body language, and making a relevant comment and asking a question. For example:

JANE:	My cat has just died.
MIKE:	Oh, that's sad. What happened?
WAYNE:	I'm going to Pizza Hut for dinner.
SARAH:	That's great. I love Pizza Hut. Who are you going with?

4 Question and discussion

 What makes you excited?

The pupils' answers to this question are written down on cards and placed in the middle of the circle. Each pupil picks up a card and has to mime it, then the others try to guess what the situation is.

The picture symbol for 'excited' is shown. Can the pupils think of other words for 'excited'? Examples are 'ecstatic', 'thrilled'.

5 Activities

The pupils interview each other in pairs and find out one thing that makes the other happy, sad and excited. These are recorded on coloured cards. The pupils also draw their perceptions of happy, sad and excited faces.

A wall display can be set up. The wall can be divided into five parts. There will be one each for happy, sad, excited and angry (to be discussed in the next session). The middle section will be a display of the picture symbols and words that mean the same. An example of this is provided.

6 Compliments and reinforcement chart

Your cat has died.	**You have won a million pounds.**
You are going to Pizza Hut for dinner.	**You have had an argument with a friend.**
You are going to the cinema.	**You have been given a certificate at school.**
You are not allowed to play with your friends.	**Your mum or dad has told you off.**
You have lost your favourite toy.	**You have bought yourself some new clothes.**

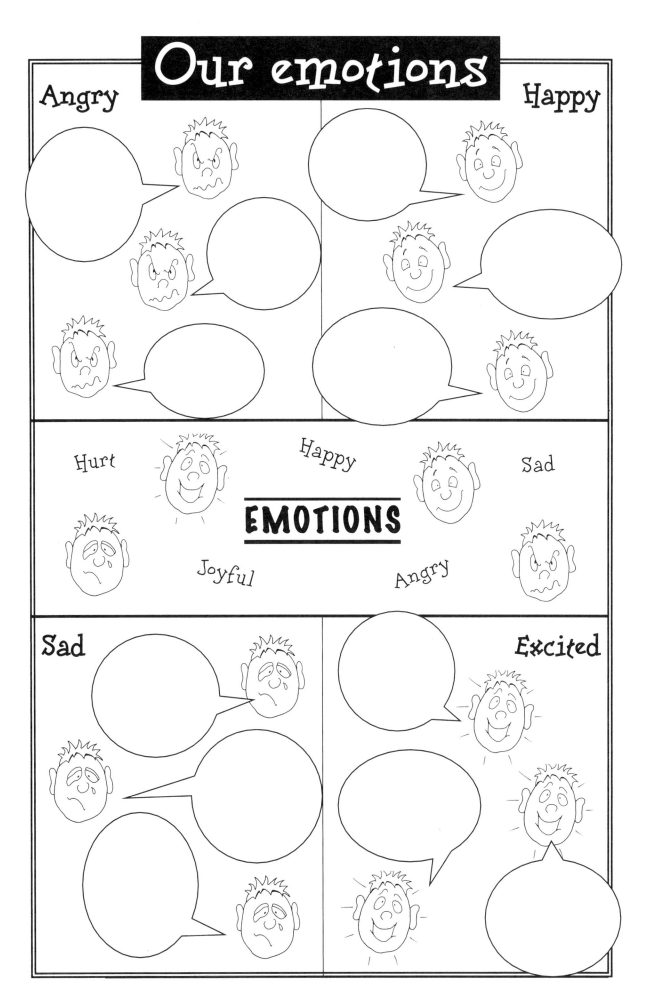

5 Anger

Equipment/Materials

Happiness chart (Session 2), picture symbols (Session 2), audio equipment, cards for second activity.

1 Greetings

The pupils are now expected to make a comment to and ask an appropriate question of the person on their left. This will be the format for greetings from now on.

JANE:	How are you feeling today?
SARAH:	I'm feeling excited because it's my birthday tomorrow.
JANE:	That's great. How old are you going to be?

This expands the pupils' skills when they greet another and teaches them how to make conversational starters, a very important technique in making and developing friendships.

2 Review

Review aims.

The happiness chart is displayed. Each pupil is given a star if they have been honest and/or have made another person happy.

3 Game – *Keep on smiling*

One person is the smiler. The rest of the pupils have unsmiling faces. The smiler looks at the person on their left and tries various ways to get them to smile. Once that person is smiling they then try to get the person on their left to smile. This continues around the circle until everyone is smiling.

4 Questions and discussion

The pupils have to ask the person on their left, 'What makes you angry?' The answers are brought back to the group for discussion.

The picture symbol for angry is shown. Can the pupils think of other words that mean the same as 'angry'? Examples are 'mad' and 'annoyed'.

Is it all right to be angry?
What do you do if you are angry?
Who do you argue with?
What do you argue about?
What is the best way of getting rid of anger? Why is this so?
What are bad ways of getting rid of anger? Why is this so?
What happens if you deal with anger incorrectly? How do you feel after this?

5 Role play

The pupils choose a situation that has made them angry. In pairs they role play two outcomes for the situation, one good and one bad. They then show this to the rest of the class. Discussion could be based on the pros and cons of each outcome.

6 Activities

The picture symbols for 'happy', 'sad', 'excited' and 'angry' are copied and each pupil receives one. The pupils will say, 'I'd like a cup of tea', expressing the emotion they have been given. This will be recorded on audio tape and then these will be played back to see if the pupils can identify and notice the difference between these emotions.

Situations that make the pupils angry are written on cards to go up on the wall display along with faces and pictures that represent anger.

7 Compliments and reinforcement chart

SESSION 6 Many emotions

Equipment/Materials

Happiness chart (Session 2),
cards for game, audio tape of
classical and modern music,
musical instruments
(optional), counters for
bingo.

1 Greetings

Include appropriate comments and questions.

2 Review

Review aims.

The happiness chart is displayed. Each pupil is given a star if they have been honest and/or have made another person happy.

3 Discussion and game

Can the pupils think of other 'feeling' words? Examples are 'joyful', 'surprised', 'nervous' and 'anxious'. Their answers are written on cards and placed in a bag. Each person takes a card out of the bag and reads the word to themselves. They must then think of a situation that would make them feel like that and, in turn, tell the others what it is. The others must guess how the pupil would feel in that situation. For example:

It's Christmas next week. How would I feel?
Excited.

4 Activity

A tape is played to the pupils. This should contain excerpts of classical and modern music that express different emotions. (This will need to be made by the teacher beforehand.) The pupils could dance to these and decide on the emotion that the music is conveying. This could be followed up by pupils using musical instruments to convey emotions.

5 **Game** – *Bingo*

Each pupil is given a bingo card that has different emotions displayed on it. The leader pulls out situation cards from a bag and reads out the situations in turn. (Both types of card are supplied for photocopying.) If the situation corresponds with an emotion on a pupil's card, then the emotion is covered with a counter. The first person to cover all the emotions on their card calls out 'Bingo'.

6 **Compliments and reinforcement chart**

You have hurt your arm.	You are late for school.	You have found a book that you thought you had lost.	Your best friend cannot come round to play.
Your favourite uncle is coming to stay at the weekend.	You can hear a creaking noise as you lie in bed.	You have come first in a race.	Your dog has run away.
You have forgotten your sister's birthday.	You have been told off when it wasn't your fault.	Your pocket money has been increased.	Someone hit you in the playground.
You have walked into a surprise birthday party for yourself.	You have a test tomorrow.	Tomorrow you are going to Disneyland.	You are not sure if you have done your homework correctly
You have to give a talk to your class.	You are new to school and don't know anybody.	You have made a new friend.	Your grandmother arrives tomorrow.
	It is your favourite lesson.	Someone called you names.	

Unit Two, Session 6 – Bingo situation cards

Unit Two, Session 6 – Bingo emotion cards

74

Unit Two, Session One

7 What is a friend?

> **Materials**
>
> Happiness chart (Session 2),
> cards for game (Session 6).

1 Greetings

Include appropriate comments and questions.

2 Question and review

Review aims. This is the last session using the happiness chart. Hopefully most of the pupils will have achieved their certificate by this time. You may want to continue so all can succeed.

Review emotions. Go around the circle and see if each pupil can name an emotion and a situation that could evoke it.

 How should we respond to certain emotions we and others have?

3 Game – *Guess the emotion*

The cards used for the previous session's discussion and game are placed in a bag (make sure you have one per person).

Each person draws out a card and has to mime the emotion. The pupils have to decide what the emotion is and say why they think it is that emotion. For example:

>> happy – smiling, body upright, eyes sparkling.

4 Question and discussion

Introduce the concept of friendship by brainstorming:

 What is a friend?

A friend could be someone who:

>> has similar interests
>> is interested in what you say
>> tells you secrets/keeps your secrets
>> invites you to do things with them
>> asks advice

>> is fun to be with
>> finds out all about you
>> plays with you
>> hugs you
>> makes you smile
>> listens to what you have to say
>> is supportive
>> helps you.

Can the pupils think of any more ideas? These should be listed and placed on a friendship chart for all to see.

Each person in the group has a turn to say who is their friend. This can be anybody, not necessarily someone in the group. Each must say why that person is their friend, using the list already mentioned. Next, each says how they themselves are a good friend to that person.

This would be a good time to introduce the friendship book and to tell the pupils what it contains and what you will be covering in this topic. Explain that there will be a friendship certificate and tell the pupils that you will be watching closely over the next few weeks and seeing who is actually being a good friend. You will be watching not only in the classroom, but in the playground and lunch hall, and during breaktime. You will also be talking to adults at home about what happens there. Only the pupils who are trying their best will be awarded the certificate.

5 Worksheet

The worksheet is the front page of the friendship book – I am a good friend. The pupils must draw a self-portrait of themselves being a good friend to others and complete the sentence 'I am a good friend because ...'.

6 Compliments and reinforcement chart

Friendship Book

I am a good friend because

SESSION 8 Friendship vouchers

1 Greetings

2 Questions and review

Review aims.

What does being a friend mean?
Who are your friends?
Why are they your friends?
What makes you a special friend?

3 Game – *Special friend*

A pupil goes out of the room. Another pupil is chosen to be a special friend, and the rest of the group have to describe the attributes of that person that make them a special friend. For example:

>> This person is caring because she looked after Tony when he fell over.
>> This person has a great sense of humour.
>> This person is close friends with Sophie.

When these attributes have been decided upon, the pupil outside is called back in. The rest of the pupils have to tell them what their special friend's attributes are and the one who was outside has to guess who it is. When they have guessed correctly, it is their special friend's turn to go outside. This continues until everybody has had a turn.

4 Question and discussion

What should friends do/not do?

Can the pupils give specific examples (without naming people) of times they have experienced or seen when someone has done something that a true friend shouldn't have done?

A list containing things friends do not do could be made and displayed next to last session's friendship chart.

5 Activity – *Friendship dominoes*

The pupils make their own friendship dominoes for their friendship book. They have to write a caption which is the opposite of the expression on the domino. (A happy face represents a good friend and an unhappy face represents someone who is not a good friend.) They then colour the faces in and stick the dominoes on card. The dominoes are put together to make a group set that can be played with. The pupils have to match each face to the appropriate situation. For example:

>> Sasha hit Tony – matches a unhappy face.
>> Lisa made Nicholas a birthday card – matches a happy face.

6 Worksheet – *Friendship voucher*

Each person chooses another's name from the names container. They must then give this person a friendship voucher. They will choose something from the friendship chart and write it down on the voucher before they give it to them. This will be discussed next session to see if the pupils have done this. The teacher will use this activity when considering the friendship certificate award at the end of this unit.

7 Worksheet – *This is my friend*

This worksheet can be done at school or home, depending on the time available.

8 Compliments and reinforcement chart

Friendship Dominoes

Unit Two, Session 8 – Friendship book, page 1

Friendship Voucher

To

For you I will

From

This is my friend

Her/his name is

_____

Things I like to do with my friend.

_____

_____

Things friends don't do together.

_____

_____

_____

9 How to make friends

Materials

Friendship vouchers
(Session 8).

1 Greetings

2 Question and review

Review aims.

 What are things friends should not do?

Discuss the friendship vouchers and ask each pupil to say honestly if they have carried out the activity fully.

3 Game – Who's speaking?

A person sits in the middle with their eyes shut. A pupil is chosen to say, 'It's bananas for dinner' in a disguised voice and the person with their eyes shut must guess who it is. When chosen correctly the person whose identity has been guessed goes into the middle and the game continues.

4 Question and discussion

 How do you make new friends?
If someone was new to your school, what would be a good way to get to know them?

Answers should include:

>> introduce yourself
>> show them around
>> smile at them
>> ask them if they would like to play with you.

 How would it feel to be new at school?
Who has felt scared and uncomfortable when they have been new to a situation?

How would you feel if someone was friendly and came up and spoke to you?

5 Role play

The pupils role play in pairs what they would do if someone were new. Both take turns at being the new person. This is then role played in front of the rest of the group.

6 Worksheet – *Making friends*

The pupils draw pictures of themselves making a new friend. They draw speech bubbles and write in them what each person might be saying.

7 Compliments and reinforcement chart

Making friends

Here are some of my friends.

When I make new friends, I ask questions
to find out about them.

Here I am finding out about

----

10 Similar interests

Materials

Picture symbols (Session 2),
friendship chart (Session 7).

1 Greetings

2 Question and review

Review aims.

How do we meet new people?
Who has been new to a situation and not known anybody?
How does it feel?
How do you get to know new people?

3 Game – *Happy feet*

The picture symbol cards are put into a container. In another container place pictures of body parts – for example, hands, feet, head and so on. (These are supplied.) Each pupil must act out the emotion using that particular body part. For example, a happy head could be the head bobbing up and down and from side to side. The rest of the pupils must guess the emotion.

4 Questions and discussion

What makes a good friend?

Review the friendship chart made in Session 7. Focus on the fact that friends have similar interests.

Can the pupils think of one thing they have in common with a friend?

Examples are:

>> music
>> going to films
>> food they both like.

How do you let someone know you like what they like?

Answers include: reflection – adding some of your own ideas; asking questions – to gain more information. For example:

> JOHN: I went to see Oasis last night.
>
> MEGAN: I love Oasis, especially their new song. Do you like it?

5 **Activity** – *Finding similar interests*

In pairs the pupils tell one another some of their interests. When the other pupil hears something that they both have in common, they then describe something from their own experience that reflects what the other has said. They also ask questions to find out more information. When one pupil has finished, the pairs swap around so that each pupil has a chance to talk about their interests as well as reflecting and questioning.

6 **Worksheet** – *Similar interests*

The pupils choose a topic that one person on their worksheet could be talking about (some ideas are given at the bottom of the worksheet). They then write what that person could be saying in their speech bubble. Next they write in the other person's bubble what they imagine that person could be saying to continue the conversation. For example:

> HANNAH: I went to see *Robin Hood* yesterday.
>
> AMY: I've seen that twice! What was your favourite part?

7 **Compliments and reinforcement chart**

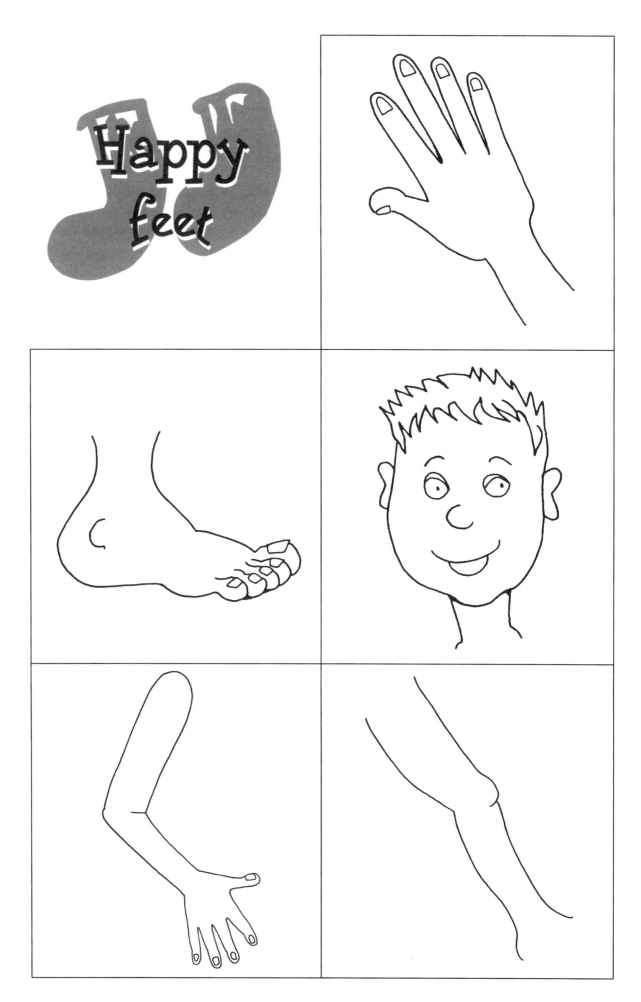

Happy feet

Unit Two, Session 10 – Body parts

Similar Interests

TOPICS

An outing   **Food**   **Films**

Books   **Playtime**   **Games**

89

SESSION 11 Keeping friends

1 Greetings

2 Questions and review

Review aims.

 How do we make new friends?
How do you let someone know that you like the same things?

Ask the pupils to name one person who is their friend and one thing they have in common with that friend.

3 Game – *Blah!*

Different friendship situations are given on the cards supplied for this session. The pupils each choose one and hold a conversation with the person on their left using words that have no meaning (e.g., 'blah'). They are allowed to use expression, body language, intonation and stress to convey the message. For example:

>> You are telling your friend that you have a tummy ache.
>> You are asking your friend if she would like to come outside and play ball.
>> You are saying sorry to a friend after having a fight.

The rest of the group try to guess the situation you are trying to convey. Discuss how they guessed it.

4 Questions and discussion

 How do you greet friends – after a short time apart?
– after a long time apart?
What do friends look like when they greet each other and/or when they are happy?

Answers should include:

>> eyes shine
>> mouth smiles
>> body is upright.

How do we keep friends?
Do friends sometimes make mistakes?
How do you make up?
Do you have to be close friends with everybody you meet?

Discuss the fact that there are people we are close to and others who are acquaintances. We do not have to be close friends with everybody. We are all different and we all have different friends.

5 Worksheet – *My friendship poem*

Read out the sample poems supplied. Explain that they are written by pupils about their friends and what friendship means to them. Encourage the pupils to write their own poems. These will be read out next session.

6 Worksheet – *Friendship questionnaire*

This is to be completed by the pupils after discussion.

7 Compliments and reinforcement chart

You are telling your friend that you have a tummy ache.	You are asking your friend if she would like to come outside and play ball.
You are saying sorry to a friend after having a fight.	You are asking a sick friend if he is feeling better.
You are comforting a friend who is unhappy.	You are giving a friend a birthday present.
You are telling a friend you are excited because you are going on holiday.	You are giving directions to your friend for getting to the shops.
You are telling your friend about a great film you went to.	You are going to share your lunch with a friend who has none.

CHRISTOPHER AND I ARE FRIENDS

by Ali

Christopher and I are friends
We play together sometimes
but not always
We talk together about cartoons such as V R Troopers
and Power Rangers
Sometimes we even have a laugh together.

FRIENDS

by Ramandeep and Rebecca

Our friends are called Atieh and Elaine
They play with us and we play babies and we play chess
We talk together about brothers and sisters.

FRIENDSHIP

by Hassan

Sometimes friends can play with each other
They can play games
They can play hide and seek and they can go to
each other's birthday parties.

My friendship poem

Friendship questionnaire

1 You have a new game. Do you ...?
(a) share it
(b) keep it to yourself
(c) give it to anybody who wants it

2 A new pupil joins your class. Do you ...?
(a) ignore them
(b) introduce yourself
(c) wait for the other pupils to go up to them

3 The new pupil is alone in the playground. Do you ...?
(a) carry on with your own game
(b) tell the teacher
(c) ask them if they would like to join in

4 How do you make a friend happy?
(a) give them a present
(b) call them names
(c) kick them when they annoy you
(d) share your toys with them
(e) help them
(f) listen to them
(g) ignore them

12 Friendship awards

Materials
Poems (Session 11).

1 Greetings

2 Review

The pupils read out the poems that they wrote in the previous session.

3 Game – *Special friend*

The game from Session 8 is played again, with a variation. The pupils should have a better understanding of this now and be able to describe personality traits instead of physical traits.

4 Activity – *Friendship certificate*

As mentioned in the introductory notes to this unit (page 47), this activity could be made into a special ceremony. Invite parents, their head teacher and other important people to the presentation. It is important that each pupil is given a reason for receiving their certificate. For example:

>> Aktar receives his certificate for playing with other pupils in the playground.

>> Louise receives her certificate for playing quietly with her sister at home and not arguing.

The pupils can colour their certificates when time permits.

5 Compliments

If you feel this would be appropriate to the situation, you could ask the pupils to give their parents, head teacher and so on a compliment, and vice versa.

Let's practise

Let's practise
– introduction

This is the third unit of Socially Speaking *'Let's practise' involves using/reinforcing the skills learnt in the previous two units, 'Let's communicate' and 'Let's be friends'.*

We spend a substantial part of our lives communicating with other people. Each time we communicate with another, either verbally or non-verbally, we have a message that we wish to convey. This message may convey one of the following:

>> greeting (e.g., 'Hello')
>> attention seeking (e.g., 'Mum!')
>> protesting, rejecting, denying (e.g., 'No, I don't want that', 'I didn't do that')
>> requesting action (e.g., 'Please give me a biscuit')
>> requesting information (e.g., 'How do I get there?')
>> stating and commenting (e.g., 'It's a nice day')
>> conversational devices (e.g., 'You'll never guess what I did!').

The type of message we convey depends greatly on the situation that we are in and the person/people we are communicating with.

Pupils with semantic/pragmatic difficulties often have difficulty in understanding the rules of interacting in social situations. They are often unaware of what they should say in the situation they are in and according to the people they are with.

For example, Craig is having dinner at a friend of his family's. When served with his meal, he says, 'Yuck, this is disgusting.' Craig obviously does not understand the rules of eating at another's place and therefore needs to be taught more acceptable responses, such as, 'Would you mind if I don't have any cabbage?' We need to teach rules so that the pupils can acquire appropriate language and behaviours that are essential for everyday life.

Skills developed

Teaching these rules requires building on the skills learnt in the previous two units and transferring them into everyday life situations. This is done through discussion, practice, role playing and experience of real life situations. The pupils thereby develop a greater understanding of themselves and the world in which they belong.

This unit also aims to develop the children's language so that it is effective – that is, appropriate and meaningful to the situation. Skills that are highlighted are:

>> giving appropriate information
>> initiating/terminating a conversation
>> taking turns
>> maintaining a topic
>> giving/taking messages.

1 Giving appropriate information

This is the ability to convey the message that is appropriate to the time, place and situation. The speaker needs to use the correct amount and type of information so that the listener is able to interpret the message meaningfully. For example:

I went to my friend Sonya's house yesterday for dinner.

This appears to be giving the appropriate amount and type of information for the listener to interpret. Now consider:

I went there.

This does not give enough information and leaves the listener unable to interpret the message. A detailed version is:

I got home and went for a shower, and then I couldn't decide what to wear. I mean, what colour really suits me best? I just don't know. Anyway I decided on red as Sonya hasn't seen my new outfit. I was in a rush when I left the house, but she lives just down the road and I

thought I had just enough time to stop at the corner shop to buy some chocolates ...

This contains far too much unnecessary information that the listener does not need to know to interpret the message being conveyed – that is, that the speaker went to Sonya's for dinner.

2 Initiating/terminating a conversation

This requires the skill of knowing when and how to initiate/terminate a conversation. Some situations are easier than others because they have a certain format to follow. For example, a telephone conversation is initiated by a greeting and terminated by a farewell. Other situations require initiating a topic that relates to a previous topic or giving a warning that the topic is going to change; for example, 'I know this off the topic but ...'.

For some pupils terminating a conversation means just turning or walking away. This is not accepted by most people and can be seen as being rude. We must teach skills of ending conversation with farewells and conversational devices such as, 'Must go' and 'I'm running late, I'd best be off.'

3 Taking turns

This has been an ongoing skill taught throughout this programme and it will be extended into real-life situations. Turn-taking requires the listener to listen to the speaker and respond appropriately to the topic introduced. This involves ability to remember the information from the previous turn and to process that information. Both participants (depending on the situation) should have an equal partnership in turn-taking (i.e., speaking and listening to each other).

4 Maintaining a topic

This requires a shared focus of attention on the part of all involved, so that the topic is maintained over a number of turns.

5 Giving/taking messages

The ability to give messages requires that the speaker takes into account the needs of the listener. Ideally, the message should be precise so that the listener can recall all of the information, and it should contain all the information necessary for the listener to know exactly what to do.

Every day, both at home and school, there are situations that require specific language and behaviours. For example, inviting a friend to play can require the following skills:

>> asking for permission from your parents
>> initiating conversation with a friend
>> giving the appropriate amount of information
>> giving precise information (e.g., where and when you want them to come)
>> listening and responding appropriately to your friend's response
>> taking turns in conversation
>> looking at your friend
>> looking/sounding interested.

During this unit the pupils will work specifically on developing telephone skills and eating out/socialising skills. But it is hoped that the pupils will be able to use skills already learnt in social situations at home, in school and in the community. Each pupil will have a specific social aim, as in 'Let's be friends', but this aim will be targeted for a week and will be evaluated during the following session. The weekly aim will be written on a voucher that will be copied; an example is provided in Session 1. One copy will be taken home and the other displayed in the classroom so that the pupil is encouraged to try to achieve the skill in both situations.

For example, Alice's aim is to ask appropriate questions. Over the week both home and school

will support Alice in achieving this aim. If others at home and school feel she has achieved this aim satisfactorily, the vouchers are then signed so that in the following session she can swap the vouchers for a sticker to go on her assessment/evaluation chart. If not, she tries again for the following week.

This requires home/school liaison, which could be introduced to parents in a meeting. This meeting would explain the aims of the term, so that everybody was clear about their role and everybody was working together. Using everyday situations and opportunities that arise at home and school will improve the pupils' communication skills overall.

Telephone

We use the telephone for many reasons including:

>> to have a chat
>> to find out information
>> to plan/book events
>> to inform others
>> to get help in an emergency situation.

The first six sessions of 'Let's practise' involve using the telephone. This requires many skills including:

>> knowing one's own telephone number
>> opening/closing telephone conversations
>> taking turns at the appropriate points
>> listening to speakers
>> giving/taking messages
>> asking/giving relevant questions/information
>> finding out information, including services that are available
>> knowing what to do in an emergency situation.

This section requires a lot of role playing using telephones. It is essential that you have some pretend telephones available. Later the pupils will need to use a real telephone and answerphone.

At the beginning of each session the pupils are encouraged to remember their telephone numbers. These are displayed to aid recall.

Discussion and role playing take place regarding appropriate ways to answer the telephone, how to ring up and speak to someone and how to call someone to the telephone. These all require specific types of language. For example:

SPEAKER A: Hello.

SPEAKER B: Hello.

SPEAKER A: Is James there, please?

SPEAKER B: Hold on a minute, I'll just get him for you.

This is then extended to giving and taking messages if the person required is not at home. It is extremely important that the message given contains relevant and specific information. The person who receives the message must be given enough information to be able to follow the message through. For example, 'Can you tell Jane to meet Kerry before school at Jane's house?' is more easily understood than 'Tell her to meet me here.'

The person receiving the message should write it down if possible, or repeat the message back orally to aid recall and memory.

In today's society there are many other modern forms of communication, such as the answerphone, fax, E-mail, pager and so on. The pupils will learn to use an answerphone as this is a communication device that they are probably going to encounter. Once again, it is important to keep language relevant to the situation and recognise what information is necessary and what is redundant. Using an answerphone is particularly good for this as there is a limited amount of time in which the pupils can speak.

Discussion takes place about what kind of message is required on an answerphone and what information should be given when a message is left. This involves practical use of an answerphone and feedback when the messages are played back.

The telephone is also used to find out information, and to plan and book events. The pupils think about certain situations that can occur and whom it would be appropriate to ring for help. The pupils put themselves in someone else's shoes whilst role playing these situations and predict what that person would say and do.

The last session of the telephone section is making emergency phone calls. The pupils need to learn:

>> the emergency telephone number
>> what service is required according to the situation
>> the need to give specific and accurate information
>> the knowledge that this number is only ever to be used in emergencies.

Cafe

The last six sessions of this unit extend the pupils' communication skills into real social contexts, those of a cafe/fast food restaurant and a tea party.

Before the pupils go to the cafe/fast food restaurant they carry out activities and role plays to enable them to gain confidence. It is suggested that within the classroom a cafe is created. This will be a co-operative task that will require both home and school to participate. The cafe has a menu that changes daily and is created by the pupils, drawing if appropriate on different nationalities and tastes within the group to reflect different cuisines. The menus can be created by using recipe books that are on display and by using the expertise of the pupils and their families.

You could request that the pupils bring in favourite music tapes from home. Each day, as the restaurant changes its cuisine, its background music can then be changed. Where appropriate, this will reflect the different cultures featured.

Decide together on a name for your restaurant, where in the classroom you would like to put it and what decor you would prefer.

On one wall there will be paper plates with the dishes of the day, made in Session 7. In the middle of the cafe a table and chairs need to be set up. The pupils can take turns at setting the table, using a tablecloth, knives and forks, glasses and so on.

Once the cafe is set up, it can be used by the pupils during the sessions and for free play. Role plays are undertaken with the pupils grouped in threes, one being the waiter/server and the others being the customers. The skills highlighted for this unit (see page 102) will need to be pointed out. For example, make sure that the pupils take turns and listen/look at the person who is talking.

The pupils also role play going to a fast food restaurant. This is practised for the following session, when they will actually go and order food themselves. Before the role plays are undertaken, a checklist is made of communicative skills needed. For example:

>> give eye contact
>> take turns
>> listen
>> give appropriate information
>> be polite
>> keep on task (talk must be relevant, no fiddling etc.).

It is important that throughout this programme the pupils always use the correct polite forms of speech for the situation.

The role plays are recorded on video and then played back to the whole group. The pupils decide what skills from the checklist were shown. It is hoped that each will be able to identify a communication skill within themselves on the video.

During the visit to the fast food restaurant adult assistance should be minimal. The pupils themselves will greet the waiter/server, give the appropriate information and pay for the food.

The final session of the unit is a tea party set up by the pupils. Once again, maximum independence is the aim. The pupils decide what is needed, who will be invited, what will be written on the invitations and where they will

have the party. Each will have one guest that they invite and take responsibility for.

Role plays take place beforehand so the pupils know what they need to say and do. For example:

>> greeting their guest
>> directing their guest where to sit
>> asking their guest what they would like to drink
>> finding out how their guest has their drink
>> giving their guest a drink
>> sitting down next to their guest and having a chat.

Finally, the pupils fill in an evaluation form which considers what they are good at, what they need to improve in and where they need help. This gives you and the pupil an idea of where they are at and what help they need in the future.

Conclusion

This unit is very practical. It gives pupils with semantic/pragmatic difficulties experience of appropriate ways to interact with people in various social situations.

As a teacher or therapist you must give these pupils opportunities to extend their skills after this programme has been completed. You should encourage them to interact with peers and adults in a variety of situations and contexts. Examples are shopping, using public transport, borrowing something, asking for help/clarification, asserting rights and so on.

You should allow the pupils to gain independence through this unit – that is, they should plan, organise, carry out and evaluate their own activities. To enable this to happen you must stand back, letting them do things for themselves and solve their own problems. Often it is all too easy to talk and do things for the pupils, but if we want them to succeed in everyday life we must give them the skills and the opportunity to try them out.

Let's practise
assessment/evaluation

Pre-unit   Post-unit

	Skills	I need help	I can do this in the classroom	I can do this out of the classroom
	TELEPHONE I know my telephone number			
	Date			
	I know how to answer the telephone			
	Date			
	I know how to ask for someone on the telephone			
	Date			
	I know how to give a message to a person			
	Date			
	I know how to leave a message on an answerphone			
	Date			
	I know how to take a message			
	Date			
	I know how to make a call when I need assistance or information (e.g. doctor, bank)			
	Date			
	I know the emergency telephone number			
	Date			
	I know who to ask for when there is a fire			
	Date			
	I know who to ask for when there is an accident			
	Date			

Let's practise
assessment/evaluation

Pre-unit   Post-unit

	Skills	I need help	I can do this in the classroom	I can do this out of the classroom
	TELEPHONE *contd*			
	I know who to ask for when there is a robbery Date			
	I can role play using a telephone Date			
	CAFE			
	I can greet the waiter/server Date			
	I can look at the waiter/server Date			
	I can ask for what I need Date			
	I can give appropriate information Date			
	I can listen to what the waiter/server says Date			
	I can respond to what the waiter/server says Date			
	I can thank the waiter/server Date			
	I can say goodbye to the waiter/server Date			

Let's practise assessment/evaluation

Pre-unit   Post-unit

	Skills	I need help	I can do this in the classroom	I can do this out of the classroom
	CAFE *contd*			
	I can role play going to a cafe			
	Date			
	TEA PARTY			
	I can greet my guest			
	Date			
	I can look at my guest when they are talking			
	Date			
	I can look at my guest when I am talking (this does not need to be all of the time)			
	Date			
	I can ask my guest appropriate questions			
	Date			
	I can start a conversation with my guest			
	Date			
	I can keep talking on the same topic			
	Date			

Relevant information:

1 Review

Materials

Cards for recording telephone numbers.

---

1 Greetings

2 Questions and review

Discuss with the pupils that their aim needs to be achieved over the week, both at home and at school. Explain the voucher system (a voucher is provided) and how the stickers are obtained for their assessment/evaluation charts.

Review all aspects of being a good communicator:

>> eye contact
>> body position
>> showing interest
>> taking turns
>> joining in with others
>> using a good voice.

 What is a friend?
What should friends do/not do?
How do you make friends?

3 Game – *Special friend*

The game from Unit Two, Session 8 is played again to reacquaint the pupils with the skills they have learnt.

4 Discussion and activity

Discussion takes place with the pupils to inform them of the programme for this term's unit. (See the introduction to this unit, page 102.)

Before the session make sure you have the pupils' telephone numbers with you in case they need help in remembering them. Ask the pupils to tell you their telephone numbers. Record the numbers on pieces of card and place them into a bag – adults should put theirs in too. You may have to help the pupils remember their numbers. Then, going around the circle, each person pulls out a telephone number and reads it aloud. The person whose telephone number it is must then put their hand up.

5 Worksheet and activity – *Ringing my friends*

Each pupil is given their telephone number to aid their memory. The pupils need to find out the telephone numbers of the rest of the group and record them on the worksheet. They must remember to use all the skills previously learnt, such as eye contact, turn-taking and so on.

Each pupil fills in their telephone number on the telephone worksheet, which is then displayed on the wall.

6 Compliments

MY AIM FOR THIS WEEK IS

Find out your friends' phone numbers

My friends' names	Telephone numbers
------------------------------	------------------------------------
------------------------------	------------------------------------
------------------------------	------------------------------------
------------------------------	------------------------------------
------------------------------	------------------------------------

2 Telephone calls

Equipment/Materials

Cards with telephone numbers (Session 1), pretend telephones.

1 Greetings

2 Questions and review

Review the aims set in the previous session.

Read out the pupils' telephone numbers again.

Can they recognise their own telephone number?

Can they say their telephone number aloud?

3 Game – *Who is in the cupboard?*

One pupil goes out of the room. Whilst they are out another pupil hides somewhere in the room (e.g., in a cupboard). The first pupil comes back in and guesses who is missing. When they have guessed correctly, the pupil who was hiding goes out of the room and the game continues.

4 Questions and discussion

Why do we use the telephone?

Answers should include:

>> to have a chat

>> to find out information

>> to plan/book events

>> to inform others.

Who do the pupils ring?

What was the last telephone call they made about?

What is the best time to ring a friend?

What do you say when you answer the telephone at home?

Brainstorm different responses. For example:

> Hello.
> Hello, Sam speaking.
> Hello, 889 9267.

 What do you say when you ring up to speak to a friend?

Brainstorm different responses. For example:

> Hello, is Michael there, please?
> Hello, it's Debbie speaking. Is Michael there, please?
> Hello, could I speak to Michael, please?

 What would you say if someone rang up and asked for your mother?

Brainstorm different responses. For example:

> Hold on, I'll just get her.
> Just a minute, I'll go and find her.

5 Role play

Split the group into subgroups (the number depends on the size of your group; there should be three or four pupils in each subgroup). There should be a divider between the subgroups so that they cannot see but can hear one other. Each subgroup should have a pretend telephone.

Each pupil is going to pretend to ring up a member of another subgroup. They dial that pupil's telephone number on a pretend phone. The person who answers should not be the pupil wanted, so that the one who answers can learn to say, 'Wait a minute, please, I'll just get her/him for you.' For example:

> Hello, Susan speaking.
> Hello, it's Sarah here. Can I please speak to Lee.
> Wait a minute, please, I'll just get him for you.
> [mouth away from telephone] Lee, Sarah is on the telephone for you.

Continue until all the pupils have had a turn at both calling someone and answering the telephone.

6 Worksheet – *Answering the telephone*

The pupils write down their responses to the opening lines on the worksheet.

7 Compliments

Telephone number _____

What would you say?

Hello,
I would like to
speak to Sophia.

Who is speaking?

- -

I am sorry,
they are not at
home.

- -

- -

SESSION 3 Messages

Equipment

Pretend telephone (optional).

1 Greetings

2 Questions and review

Going around the circle, each person recalls their phone number.

Why do we use the telephone?
What do you say when you answer the phone?
What do you say if you are ringing up someone?

3 Game – *Ring, ring*

This game is similar to the role play in Session 2, except that it is done in a circle. The teacher starts and rings up the person on her/his left, requesting that s/he may speak to the next person to the left in the circle. This can be mimed or a pretend telephone can be used. It continues person by person until everyone in the circle has had a turn.

4 Questions and discussion

What do you say if the person is not at home?

Brainstorm different responses. For example:

> They're not at home at the moment.
> Sorry, they've just gone out.
> They can't come to the phone right now.
>> (Pupils should be encouraged to use answers similar to the last one if they are alone.)

How would you leave a message?

Brainstorm different responses. For example:

> Can I leave a message?
> Could you tell them that ...

It is important that the message is clear and that it contains the relevant information. For example:

>> name of the caller
>> why they rang
>> a contact phone number if necessary.

Some pupils find it very difficult to give specific information. For example, they may say, 'Tell her that he should meet me there.' This does not give enough information for the person receiving the message to be able to follow it through. The pupils should be encouraged to repeat the message back to aid recall and memory.

5 Role play

The pupils are divided into subgroups of three people. One person is the caller, another will answer the phone and the third person will be the one whom the message is for. The role play should follow these lines. The third person should be out of hearing to start with.

JOHN: Hello, John speaking.
FIONA: Hello, it's Fiona speaking. Is Kirk there, please?
JOHN: I'm sorry, he's not home at the moment.
FIONA: Can I leave a message, please?
JOHN: Wait a minute, I'll just get a pen ... OK, I'm ready.
FIONA: Can you tell him that Fiona rang and that he needs to bring his Take That CD to school tomorrow?
JOHN: He needs to bring his Take That CD to school tomorrow. OK.
FIONA: Thanks. Bye.
JOHN: Goodbye.

The third pupil then comes along and John gives them the message. Pupils who cannot write will need to remember the message and pass it on orally.

All of the role plays are performed in front of the rest of the main group as a small play. You will need to give ideas for messages if the pupils cannot think of their own.

6 Worksheet – *Can I take a message?*

The pupils write down the message on their message pad.

7 Homework – *Ring a friend*

Divide the pupils into pairs. Each pupil will be given a message to ring up and give to their partner. Messages are provided. That night each must ring up the other to give the message.

8 Compliments

Could you tell her that Mike rang and could she bring her new video to school tomorrow?

Becky is not home at the moment. Can I take a message?

1 Who is the message for?

2 Who rang?

3 What is the message?

Can I take a message?

Ask your mum or dad if you can ring _____
to give them a message.

The message is:

'Bring a toy to school on Monday.'

Ask your mum or dad if you can ring _____
to give them a message.

The message is:

'Bring a book to school on Monday.'

SESSION 4 Answerphone

Equipment	Preparation
Pretend telephone (optional), answerphone or taped answerphone message.	Suitable arrangements need to be made in advance for the answerphone activity.

1 Greetings

2 Questions and review

Review the aims from the previous session.

Go around the circle. Each person recalls their telephone number.

What do you say when you answer the telephone?
What do you say if you are ringing up someone?
What do you say if a person is not at home?
How would you leave a message?

3 Game – *They're not at home*

This is similar to the game in Session 3: Ring, ring. Either mime or use a pretend telephone. The teacher starts by ringing up the person on her/his left, asking to speak to their mother/father or sibling. The pupil must answer, 'I'm sorry, they're not at home. Can I take a message?' The teacher gives a simple message which the pupil repeats back. Continue this around the circle.

4 Questions and discussion

What happens if no one is at home when you ring?

Brainstorm ideas. For example:

>> no one answers
>> they may have an answerphone that turns on.

Why do people have answerphones?
When would they turn one on?
Who has an answerphone at home?

Discuss why people have answerphones – to receive messages when they are out or unable to answer their phones. You could mention other modern forms of communication such as fax, E-mail, pagers and so on.

Listen to an answerphone message. You may want to bring in an answerphone or tape the message on one and play it to the pupils.

 What information should people have in their message?

Brainstorm ideas. For example:

>> a greeting
>> name and/or telephone number
>> a special message
>> an instruction about how to leave a message
>> an ending.

What information should people give when they leave a message?

Brainstorm ideas. For example:

>> a greeting ('Hello')
>> an introduction ('It's Jay here')
>> a message ('I'll meet you outside McDonalds at 12.30')
>> an ending ('See you later').

Depending on the age and level of your group, you may want to discuss the difference between a formal message (left with someone you don't know or relating to a business call) and an informal message (left with someone you know well).

5 Activity

The pupils think of messages that they could give to a friend. Once again, brainstorm ideas that they could use for messages. For example:

>> Meeting to go shopping, for a drink, to see a film and so on.
>> Asking if their friend would like to come round to play.
>> Reminding them of something they are supposed to do.

While the pupils are filling in the worksheet, one by one they go and ring up an answerphone and leave a message. (Hopefully an adult within the group will have an answerphone that could be used; or a parent may be willing to help.) These messages could either be stored on the answerphone or taped onto an audio tape so that they can be played back at the next session.

6 Worksheet – *Answerphone*

The pupils write their answerphone messages down on the worksheet.

7 Compliments

Please leave a message.

Please leave your name and number.

Wait for the beep.

I am not at home.

What message would you put on your answerphone?

_____

_____

_____

5 Who do I ring?

Equipment

Taped messages from previous session.

1 Greetings

2 Question and review

Review the aims from the previous session.

Go around the circle. Each person recalls their telephone number.

 What information should people leave when they are giving a message on an answerphone?

Play back the answerphone messages from the previous session and check to see if people gave the correct information.

3 Game – *Who am I?*

Each pupil is given one of the occupation cards provided. They try to mime what that person does so that the others can guess who they are. The teacher may need to model this at first.

4 Questions and discussion

Show the occupation cards. Display two or three pictures at a time and ask, 'Who would you ring if ...?'

For example, show pictures of a doctor, dentist and electrician:

 Who would I ring if I had toothache?
Who would I ring if all my lights didn't work?
Who would I ring if I had a tummy ache?

5 Role play

The pupils are divided into pairs and each pair is given an occupation card. One takes on the role of that occupation and the other has to call them (or their receptionist) to make an appointment. You may have to model one situation to give the pupils help to start. See if they can do the role plays by themselves with no adult help. These are then performed in front of the rest of the class.

6 Worksheet – *Who can I ring?*

The pupils match the phone numbers on the worksheet to the situations.

7 Compliments

Occupations

Electrician

Doctor

Dentist

Travel agent

Plumber

Builder

What phone number do you ring?

Baker	**0181 866 2057**
Bank	**0181 940 7104**
Dentist	**0171 828 0561**
Doctor	**0171 437 0722**
Electrician	**0181 954 2335**
Railway station	**0181 503 6297**

1 Your lights have gone out
and you cannot see. --

2 You want to find out how much
you have in your savings account. ----------------------------

3 You need to find out what time
your train goes to Brighton. ----------------------------------

4 You have a sore throat
and a runny nose. --

5 You have toothache. --

6 You need to order bread
and cakes for a party. --

SESSION 6 Emergency

<table>
<tr><td>

Equipment

Occupation cards (Session 5).

</td><td>

Preparation

Pictures from newspapers of emergencies.

</td></tr>
</table>

1 Greetings

2 Question and review

Review the aims from the previous session.

Go around the circle. Each person recalls their telephone number.

 Who would you ring if you had toothache?

Use all the occupation cards, asking similar questions.

3 Game – *Can you help?*

Each person is given a situation card (these are provided) and an occupation card. You may need to photocopy the occupation pictures so you have enough for everyone. The teacher starts off by telling the person on her/his left a situation: 'I have toothache. Can you help?' If that person has the dentist card they say 'Yes'; if not, they say 'No'. The teacher continues around the circle until s/he finds the person who can help. That person then asks the person on their left a question that relates to their situation to see if they can help. Continue until all have had a turn.

4 Questions and discussion

 What is an emergency?
What telephone number do you ring in an emergency?

Show pictures of emergencies; for example, a fire, a car accident, a robbery.

 Who would you ask for if there was a fire?
Who would you ask for if there was an accident?
Who would you ask for if there was a robbery?

Stress that the emergency number should only ever be rung in an emergency, never at any other time.

5 Role play

Divide the pupils into subgroups, each with an adult. If there is only one adult then this will be done as a whole class activity. Each pupil is given a picture of an emergency. The adult plays the part of the 999 operator, and the pupils take turns to ring 999 and ask for the service they require. For example:

TEACHER:	Emergency Services. Which service do you require?
PUPIL:	Ambulance.
TEACHER:	Ambulance Service. What is your name?
PUPIL:	Kevin Logan.
TEACHER:	What is your address?
PUPIL:	44 Banks Avenue, Chiswick, London.
TEACHER:	What is your phone number?
PUPIL:	0181 997 8657
TEACHER:	What has happened?
PUPIL:	A car has crashed into a pole outside my house and the driver is unconscious.
TEACHER:	An ambulance is on its way.

6 Worksheet – *What would you say?*

The pupils write down their responses to the operator's questions on the worksheets.

7 Compliments

Situation cards

You have toothache.	You need to have a dental check-up.
Your lights have all gone out.	None of your plugs and sockets is working.
You have the flu.	You have hurt your leg badly.
A pipe in your house is leaking.	Your kitchen tap will not turn off.
You want to have a wall built around your house.	You want to build a new room on to your house.
You want to book a holiday to France.	You need to find out the price of an air ticket.

EMERGENCY

1 'Which service do you want?'

_____

2 'What is your name?'

_____

3 'Where are you?'

_____

4 'What has happened?'

_____

_____

EMERGENCY

Fire Service

Ambulance Service

Police

1 'Which service do you want?'

----

2 'What is your name?'

----

3 'Where are you?'

----

4 'What has happened?'

EMERGENCY

1 'Which service do you want?'

_____

2 'What is your name?'

_____

3 'Where are you?'

_____

4 'What has happened?'

_____

_____

SESSION 7 Our cafe

<table>
<tr><td>

Materials

Paper plates, materials for pretend food.

</td><td>

Preparation

Pupils should be asked to bring recipe books for this session; see the introductions to this unit (page 104).

</td></tr>
</table>

1 Greetings

2 Questions and review

Review the aims from the previous session.

Go around the circle. Each person recalls their telephone number.

What is an emergency?
What telephone number do you ring in an emergency?
What would you ask for if there was a fire?
What would you ask for if there was an accident?
What would you ask for if there was a robbery?

3 Game – *Making a cup of tea*

This is a sequencing game. The teacher starts with the first step of making a cup of tea. Each person in turn says what the next step is until the tea is made. For example:

> I put some water in the kettle.
> Next I plug the kettle in.
> Next, I put some tea bags in a teapot.

You may need to act this out using real objects if the pupils find the task particularly difficult.

4 Questions and discussion

Look together at recipe books that the pupils have brought into school. If appropriate, make a list of the different nationalities relating to food that these books include. Discuss the fact that many restaurants serve food from different cultures, usually because of the tastes and cultures of the people owning/managing them.

What types of food do the pupils eat at home?
What is each person's favourite food?

If you have many cultures represented within your group, it would be a good idea to look at the food specialities of each culture and to raise once again the fact that we are all different and have different tastes.

Introduce the plan that the group is going to make their own restaurant, a restaurant that changes its menu daily. Each pupil is going to choose a restaurant that relates to a particular nationality or culture; for example, a fast food restaurant, an Indian restaurant, a French restaurant. If possible, use the expertise of the pupils and their parents to create menus.

You could also ask the pupils to bring favourite music tapes or CDs from home. If appropriate, these could reflect their own culture. Each day as the restaurant changes its cuisine, it also changes its background music.

Decide on a name for your restaurant, where in the classroom you will put it and what decor you will have.

5 Activity

Using junk materials and paper plates, the pupils can make a meal from their menu. Find a variety of materials to represent foods so they can use their imagination and creativity. The pupils can stick the meals on plates, and these could be put on one side of the restaurant as a 'dish of the day' display.

6 Worksheet – *Menu*

Show the pupils the worksheet and highlight the two types of course included. Check that the pupils can differentiate between the courses.

Using the recipe books, the pupils decide what meals and drinks they will have on their menu and the price for them. This will be completed in the next session.

7 Homework

The pupils should collect information about their family's favourite foods, including the cost of them, in readiness for the next session.

8 Compliments

MENU

Main courses

£ _____

£ _____

£ _____

£ _____

Desserts

£ _____

£ _____

£ _____

£ _____

Drinks

£ _____

£ _____

£ _____

£ _____

SESSION 8 Let's eat

1 Greetings

2 Questions and review

Review the aims from the previous session.

 What were we making last week?
What is the name of our cafe?
What are the types of food our cafe will have?

3 Game – *I went to our cafe*

This is similar to 'I went shopping' in Unit One, Session 7. The pupils add on items of a menu. For example:

A: I went to our cafe and ate spaghetti.

B: I went to our cafe and ate spaghetti and chicken curry.

Continue around the circle and see if everyone can remember the sequence.

4 Worksheet – *Menu*

The order of this session is different from usual so that the menus started in Session 7 can be completed and role play can take place afterwards. When the menus are finished they can be put into folders, and the pupils can design the covers. They may want to use computer graphics, magazine pictures or their own drawings.

5 Role play

It is hoped that by the time this session is held, the cafe will be completed or nearly completed. A table or tables are set up with cutlery, plates and glasses and so on. The pupils are grouped in threes, two being the customers and one being the waitress/waiter. They practise using their menus and ordering their food. The cafe is then used as a stage and the role play is performed to the rest of the group. You may want to use pretend food, or even the plates of food made in Session 7.

After each role play you should reinforce all the skills the pupils have displayed; for example, eye contact, turn-taking, listening and so on. (These should be continually reinforced throughout the whole unit.)

The cafe should be accessible to the pupils throughout the rest of the term for free play. Remember to change the menu each day and, if possible, the music. You may want to decide on a time each day when music is playing.

6 Compliments

Equipment/Materials

Table, real or pretend food
types, cutlery, plates and so
on; pretend menu; video
equipment.

1 Greetings

2 Questions and review

Review the aims from the previous session.

*What does a waitress/waiter say to people who have just sat
down in a restaurant or cafe?*
What courses could you order?
When do you pay in a restaurant or cafe?
What should you always remember to say to staff in cafes?
(Please, thank you)

3 Game – *Pass the salt*

A table is set up in the middle of the circle with various food types – actual or pretend – and
cutlery and utensils on it. The teacher turns to the pupil on her/his left and asks if they would
pass certain items. The number of items requested will depend on the capabilities of your
pupils. For example:

> Jane, would you please pass me the apple, the biscuits and the
> lemonade.

The pupils should repeat the items back to aid retention. Continue around the circle.

4 Questions and discussion

Display on the wall a pretend menu for a fast food restaurant – for example, McDonalds).
Discuss the items on the menu and their prices.

What do you like to eat when you go out for a hamburger?
How do you order your food? At a table or counter?
What do you say when you order your food?

5 Role play

The teacher assumes the role of serving the pupils at a fast food restaurant. A table is set up and the menu displayed. Each pupil has a turn at coming in and ordering something from the menu. For example:

PUPIL: Hello.

TEACHER: Hello, how can I help you?

PUPIL: I would like a cheeseburger and french fries, please.

TEACHER: A cheeseburger and french fries, is that to eat here or take away?

PUPIL: Eat here, please.

TEACHER: That will be £2.10, please.

Both the pupil and the teacher should mime the giving of money and food and so on.

6 Activity – *Video*

Before the video is made, the pupils and the teacher make a checklist of things they must remember to do. You may want to take photographs inside a fast food restaurant beforehand to use as a stimulus. For example:

>>   make eye contact
>>   take turns
>>   listen
>>   give appropriate information
>>   be polite
>>   keep on task (talk is relevant, no fiddling etc.)

In subgroups of three, the pupils role play a fast food restaurant. One is the server and the other two order food. The teacher videos this, and the videos are played back to the full group. Each video is discussed positively with regard to the checklist. Can the pupils identify good communication skills in themselves?

7 Discussion

Introduce the idea that in the following session the pupils are going to go to a real cafe/fast food restaurant. Once again, go over the checklist to reinforce the skills that they will need to use on this trip.

You can choose your destination according to convenience, accessibility and what you feel your pupils can handle. A letter will need to be sent to parents informing them of the intention to hold the trip and the likely cost.

8 Compliments

10 Let's go out

1 Greetings

2 Review

Review the aims from the previous session.

Before you go out, review the checklist made in Session 9. You might want to give each pupil an individual aim from this list to achieve during the trip.

3 Activity

The aim of this outing is to give the pupils as much communicative independence as possible. They should greet the waiter/server themselves, order the food, give appropriate information and pay for the food. Adults should assist only when needed.

4 Evaluation

This will need to be done as soon as possible after the trip. Ask the pupils what they felt about this experience. Highlight on the checklist the skills that each pupil showed. Together with the teacher, the pupils should think of any areas with which they still need help.

5 Compliments

SESSION 11 Invitations

1 Greetings

2 Question and review

Review the aims from the previous session.

What do you need to remember when you are ordering food in a cafe?

Once again, reinforce the checklist made in Session 9.

3 Game – *Eating out*

A pile of cards is placed in the middle of the circle (cards are provided). These show behaviour that is not acceptable in social situations. The teacher picks one up and orders food from the next person, displaying the inappropriate behaviour on the card. For example:

> CARD 1:   Do not say 'please' and 'thank you'.
> TEACHER: Give me a hamburger.

The pupils must decide what the unacceptable behaviour is. Then the next pupil picks up a card. For example:

> CARD 2:   Do not look at the person you are talking to.
> PUPIL: Please can I have a hamburger. [no eye contact]

4 Questions and discussion

Introduce the idea that the following week your group is going to give a tea party.

Who will the pupils invite?

It would be best to choose people from the school; for example, the head teacher, secretary, welfare assistants and so on.

What will you have to eat and drink?
If you are going to make tea and coffee, what items will you need to make these?
How should the classroom be set up?
What music (if any) would the pupils like in the background?

5 Role play

It would be a good idea for each pupil to invite one person each. This person could be their guest during the tea party. The situation needs to be role played. For example:

What do you say when your guest arrives?
Welcome, come and sit down.

What would be the first question you ask your guest?
What would you like to drink?

What other questions do you need to ask?
Do you take milk?
Do you take sugar?
Would you like a biscuit?

Once your guest has got a drink and some food, what should you do?

Answers should include:

Get my own drink and biscuit.
Sit down next to them and chat.

What questions could you ask them to start chatting?
What have you done today?
How is your work going?

The pupils then role play in pairs in front of the group; this is not practised first. The rest of the group should give positive remarks and constructive criticism. You may want to adapt this according to the needs and levels of your pupils.

6 Worksheet – *Invitations*

Each pupil fills in the details on their invitation (this is supplied). Discuss the relevant information that is needed on the invitation:

>> The name of the person being invited.
>> Who is having the tea party.
>> Where the party is.
>> The time of the party.
>> An RSVP.

Once they have completed this, the pupils could deliver their invitations. You may want to make some time available during the following week to rehearse the tea party and perhaps to make biscuits for it.

7 Compliments

Do not say 'please' and 'thank you'.	Do not look at the person you are talking to.
Do not smile.	Do not wait your turn.
Pretend to sneeze with no handkerchief.	Talk with your back to the person you are talking to.
Talk too loudly.	Talk too softly.
Laugh as you talk.	Pretend to chew gum with your mouth open.
Speak too quickly.	Finish what you are saying in the middle of a sentence.
Give far too much information.	Talk too slowly.

INVITATION

SESSION 12 Tea party

1 Activity – *Tea party*

The pupils will have set up the classroom before the tea party, organising all of the equipment needed. Try to let them do as much as possible by themselves. The adults should be in charge of making the hot drinks, but other than that hopefully the pupils will be fully capable of completing this activity by themselves.

2 Evaluation form

Evaluation form

I think I am good at

I have improved in

I need help in

But I am always getting better.

Bibliography

Curry M, Bromfield C

    1994   *Personal and Social Education for Primary Schools through Circle Time*. A Nasen Publication.

Glaser A, Johnson E, Derickson B

    1991   *A Sourcebook of Pragmatic Activities*. Communication Skill Builders.

ILEA

    1988   *Hello, What Next? Social Skills and Language Impaired Children*. Swindon Press Ltd.

Johnson M

    1991–1992   *Functional Communication in the Classroom*. The Manchester Metropolitan University.

Locke A

    1985   *Living Language*. NFER–Nelson.

McTear M, Conti-Ramsden G

    1992   *Pragmatic Disability in Children*. Whurr Publishers Ltd.

Mogford-Bevan K, Sadler S (Editors)

    Child Language Disability, Volume 2, *Semantic and Pragmatic Difficulties*. Multilingual Matters Ltd.

Mosley J

    1993   *Turn Your School Round*. LDA.

Rinaldi W

    1992   *The Social Use of Language Programme*. NFER–Nelson.

Spense S

    1985   *Social Skills Training with Children and Adolescents*. NFER–Nelson.